PRAISE FOR *ROBERT GRIFFIN III*

Robert Griffin III captured affections of the football faithful in the nation's capital and beyond during his wildly successful rookie year with the Washington Redskins. In this book, Ted Kluck—one of my favorite writers—provides a compelling glimpse into Griffin's life and young career. The jury is still out on Griffin's long-term impact on the NFL, but his story is certainly worth reading. Kluck has done sports fans a great service in telling it.

TIM ELLSWORTH, COAUTHOR OF
PUJOLS: MORE THAN THE GAME

"Big WE .... Little Me" —Robert's mantra for Leadership is succinctly captured within the spirit of this book.

TERRY SHEA, FORMER NFL AND COLLEGE
COACH AND QUARTERBACK MENTOR

Ted is more than a great Christian writing about sports. I think he's one of the best sportswriters period. I found his reflections on RG3 relentlessly interesting and his ruminations about faith and superstardom wise and measured.

KEVIN DeYOUNG, SENIOR PASTOR,
UNIVERSITY REFORMED CHURCH, EAST
LANSING, MI; AUTHOR OF *CRAZY BUSY*

ROBERT GRIFFIN III

ATHLETE, LEADER, BELIEVER

TED KLUCK

THOMAS NELSON
Since 1798

NASHVILLE   DALLAS   MEXICO CITY   RIO DE JANEIRO

Published in Nashville, Tennessee, by Thomas Nelson. Thomas Nelson is a registered trademark of Thomas Nelson, Inc.

Published in association with the literary agency of Wolgemuth & Associates, Inc.

Thomas Nelson, Inc., titles may be purchased in bulk for educational, business, fund-raising, or sales promotional use. For information, please e-mail SpecialMarkets@ThomasNelson.com.

Library of Congress Control Number: 2013937530

ISBN: 9781595555748

Printed in the United States of America

13 14 15 16 17 18 RRD 6 5 4 3 2 1

*For Tris and Maxim, because football is
for little boys and their dreams*

CONTENTS

FOREWORD

It's good to see good people succeed. I had the chance to spend some time with Robert Griffin III last year at an awards ceremony and found him to be a great kid with great parents. You root for people like that.

Robert and I really couldn't be more different as far as quarterbacking style and background are concerned. I grew up in a small town in Pennsylvania, whereas he played for a high school powerhouse in Texas. I was a pocket passer and ran when I had to, usually paying a huge price for it. I basically donated my body to this game, and now every time I take a step I feel it. I know that Robert knows what he's getting into, but this game at this level can take things away from a person that you can't even imagine.

There's a newness and a freshness to his game that connects with fans who are in a constant pursuit of perfection. He makes defensive players look ridiculous with his world-class speed and athletic ability. His style is fun to watch, and it's probably fun for him to execute. I think it will catch up to him eventually, but I definitely enjoy watching it.

Robert is a part of a rookie quarterback class that is taking the league by storm this year. Along with Andrew Luck and Russell Wilson, he seems to be breathing life into the position and in some ways redefining how it is played. And for now he's doing so with class and integrity. I hope and pray that his integrity continues and remains strong, as I know firsthand the kind of temptation and compromise that can come with success on an NFL stage.

Robert is taking center stage this season and is in the crosshairs of a media frenzy that extends beyond the most political city in the world. His every word and action is analyzed in more detail than at any other time in pro football history. When I think back on my years in the NFL, it was truly a different era—an era without Twitter, Facebook, and twenty-four-hour online coverage of our league and its teams. Then, there was still a private life that for the most part remained private.

What Ted has written is a respectful, thoughtful book that is not only a book on Robert Griffin but also a book on quarterbacking and faith. Ted is clearly a student of football, and his passion for the game is visible throughout these pages. He breaks down film. He crunches numbers. He takes what is in many ways a difficult subject—a rookie quarterback who is still largely unproven—and provides shape and context to what Griffin has done and what he's capable of; and he does it respectfully, with a perspective on what the men who have quarterbacked before him have done.

It's strange that we live in a world where there are books contracted on players who haven't even finished their rookie years—and, more importantly, who haven't yet faced the spiritual and emotional challenges that come with adulthood, marriage, and family or the pressures of being the long-term faces of their franchises. Ted acknowledges this strangeness honestly, but then dives headlong, joyfully, into the RG3 quarterbacking fray. With Ted, you'll learn about football on these pages, and you'll ask important spiritual questions, all in the context of a young player who is thrilling us on Sundays.

Enjoy,
Jim Kelly
NFL Hall of Fame

ON ATHLETES, HYPE, AND
FOOTBALL BOOKS

AN INTRODUCTION TO RG3

I consider myself a sort of archivist of football experiences—some meaningful to the masses, and some just meaningful to me. I remember my first live NFL game—an Indianapolis Colts exhibition game against the Houston Oilers in 1984. I hyperventilated when I walked through the concourse and saw the green Hoosier Dome AstroTurf for the first time. I would play on that field eight years later. I remember the first time I cared about my team losing—in 1985, when the Chicago Bears lost on the road to the Miami Dolphins on *Monday Night Football* and I was allowed to stay up late to watch it.

As an adult I no longer care about or cheer for teams. Rather, I'm on a search for the singular experience: for a player or team special enough to merit consideration and watchfulness. I have a houseful of these experiences. I have the Doug Williams Super Bowl on VHS. I have the entire 1985 Bears season on DVD. I have some Barry Sanders games on DVD. I have DVDs of teams (Los Angeles Express vs. New Jersey Generals, or

Steve Young vs. Doug Flutie) and leagues (remember the WLAF?) that have almost no meaning to anyone anymore, but for some reason trigger memories for me. I have a closet full of old jerseys that are themselves more of an homage to fabrics (remember Sand-Knit and Durene?) and NFL Draft Busts (remember Rashaan Salaam?) than anything quantifiably great. Football, like music, was made for archivists. It's made for that little rush of serotonin that comes from finding the perfect jersey, or the perfect old bootlegged DVD on eBay.

That's why I take the study and archival of Robert Griffin III so seriously. These will be some kid's first memories of the NFL.

We live in the kind of world where three weeks into a player's rookie season, books are already being written and speculation is already being made about a rookie player "altering the landscape of the league." While I'm resolute in thinking that this is jumping the gun, I'm also excited to be involved. As an author, I've been roped into these kinds of projects before. About a year ago, I was one of about fifty-five authors to sign to do book projects on then–New York Knicks point guard Jeremy Lin, who was a flash in the pan of epic flash-in-the-pan proportions. Seemingly the day after we all signed our contracts, Lin blew out his knee and was on the shelf for the season, but I'm still glad I did it, because I enjoyed Lin and enjoyed delving into his story.

We live in the kind of world where Tim Tebow has a documentary made about him—creepily entitled *The Chosen One*—when he is in high school and receives a high-profile book deal the moment he steps off the field after his last college game. We live in the kind of world where a book like that becomes an immediate *New York Times* best seller and makes an even bigger hero out of its subject.

So what's in it for someone like me to do a book like this, and for someone like you to read it? Well, for one, I grew up reading football books. I read great football books, like George Plimpton's *Paper Lion*; terrible books, like Jim McMahon's ghostwritten autobiography; and great books masquerading as terrible books, like the sneakily funny and insightful *The Boz* by Brian Bosworth with then relatively unknown Rick Reilly. I loved reading football books then, and I love reading them now. I also occasionally love writing them. I say "occasionally" because we also now live in a world where it's increasingly rare to get an athlete to say anything interesting that hasn't already been vetted by twenty-five PR reps and an agent before it hits the wires. We live in a world where athletes are more accessible because of Twitter and Facebook, and are therefore more ordinary, than they've ever been. I'm convinced that I loved Walter Payton *more* in 1985 because I didn't have access to his every ordinary thought via Twitter. He lived and died larger than life to me.

Here's what I endeavor to do: I hope to see and write things as an *author* would see and write things. I want to see how Griffin handles himself around his teammates. I want to see how he leads on and off the field. I want to know if the way Robert Griffin plays has a shelf life. I want to know if I'll be watching him in ten years. I want to watch every offensive snap he takes, from multiple angles.

Because at the end of the day, we still live in the kind of world where all we really know about an athlete is quantifiable production on the field. I know that in Week 3 of the 2012 NFL season, his record is 1-2, and that he's 60-89 for 747 yards, 4 TDs, and a pick passing. I know that he's added an additional 209 rushing yards and 3 TDs on the ground.

In Week 3, three of the top five stories on NFL.com this afternoon concern fines levied by the NFL for criticisms of the NFL's replacement officials—a story that's destined to become a footnote in NFL history but that is commanding headlines today. I know that in Week 3, last year's Hot Item Quarterback, Cam Newton, was shown scowling and hanging his head on the sideline during a Carolina Panthers loss—defenses seeming, for the time being at least, to have figured out his dual-threat attack. I also know that RG3 appears to do what he does with considerably more joy than Newton. I know that they are both world-class athletes, but that Griffin seems to have captured the fancy of Madison Avenue in a more significant way than the scowly Newton. It is still news for any athlete to capture Madison Avenue, which explains part of our fascination with RG3.

I know that RG3, a Heisman Trophy winner at Baylor, plays like he's in a video game, and that makes him fun to watch. I know that he made Baylor football, for a brief moment in time, matter. I know that the kids on the fourth-grade peewee football team I'm coaching all wear visors like RG3, and that the quarterback (a moonfaced white kid named RJ) refers to himself as RJ3. Strange and fun times indeed.

So consider this introduction an invitation. Consider it an invitation to enjoy football, and not an invitation to a new hero or idol, because *how* we enjoy Robert Griffin III ultimately says as much about us as it says about him.

And life being the difficult and uncertain thing that it is, I'm not sure, ultimately, what kind of a person RG3 will end up being. He's only twenty-two years old. But what's comforting in all of this is that sports, and athletes, don't exist to receive our worship; and when they do, it's always unhealthy and disappointing in the end. Rather, RG3 and football should remind us of who it is that we *really* worship. This may happen because of what an athlete says, but more often I think it happens because of how an athlete plays and conducts himself. There's something in Robert's game that suggests that God *made* him to do exactly this, exactly now. And that's an exciting thing to see.

AUTHOR'S NOTE ON
CHRONOLOGY AND VERB TENSE

I officially learned of this project on Week 3 of the 2012 NFL season, and the first draft was due before the Divisional Round of the play-offs. As such, there's a sense of *immediacy* to a lot of the writing—that is, I was writing it down as it was happening, and as Griffin himself was happening. It seemed like this kid was writing his own story from week to week, and my keyboard and I were along for the ride, trying to keep up. A lot of the game stuff is in the present tense—even the old games. I'm writing it for you as I'm *experiencing* it. The book is laid out semichronologically (high school, college, draft, etc.), but even in the old stuff there are allusions and references to what's happening today and what may happen in the future. We don't have the luxury of wistfully remembering someone as new as Griffin; newness is unfolding, it seems, every minute of every day.

Also, I do a lot of speculating as the season unfolds, because speculating is part of what's enjoyable about being a football fan and a football writer. I couldn't keep myself from asking questions throughout. Would Griffin stay healthy? Would Andy Reid keep his job? Would Rex Ryan finally bench Mark Sanchez? Chances are, if you're reading this, you already know the answers to those questions. And chances are, you didn't buy the book and aren't flipping pages furiously to find out if Reid keeps his job (he doesn't) or if Sanchez remains the starter (weirdly, he does) because those items have already been reported, oh, twelve hundred times already. My hope is that you'll enjoy the newness and freshness of Robert Griffin one more time and that there's no sense of "old news" to those questions because of how legit and immediate they were as the season unfolded. These are the things we cared about in 2012, and these are the things that provided the backdrop for the RG3 story as it unfolded before us.

I can't help but suggest and discuss a few of the resources that helped me in the writing of this book. First, if you're at all interested in NFL quarterbacking or just quarterbacking in general, you owe it to yourself to read Terry Shea's fantastic book *Eyes Up.* This is the gold standard in quarterbacking manuals, drawing on Shea's decades' worth of experience as a coach at the college and professional levels. Also, the book *Showdown* by Thomas G. Smith aided greatly in the writing of my chapter on the racial history of the Washington Redskins and is just a fascinating read anyway.

Finally, you may notice that although I admire and am enamored with young Griffin's athletic ability and charisma, I'm slow to anoint him on a football or cultural level just yet. This is because, influenced by the spirit of Timothy Keller's great book *Counterfeit Gods,* I strove to place Griffin and football in their proper context as *created* things, not as the *Creator* Himself.

1

NOBODY GETS FAMOUS BY ACCIDENT: CREATING ROBERT GRIFFIN III

B eing a military kid, I was blessed to live a life that's hard to put into words," Griffin Tweeted about his parents. "Discipline. Perseverance. Respect are a start . . . ," the Tweets continued. "Yet those words are so much more than words in the lives of those who serve & their children. More than an inspirational quote on the wall. . . . They are life. Life [b]ecause it takes a life of discipline, perseverance & respect to have the willingness to dedicate your life to serve. . . . As a kid I experienced this dedication, as many friends saw their parents come back from war . . . and many didn't. . . . Those who serve, both past and present, change lives forever. They risk changing the lives of their wives and children to protect us all. . . . So as a kid I thought my Heroes were fictional characters or professional athletes, but now I realize who my real heroes are. . . . The men and women who have stood, are still standing, and have fallen so that we may live our lives free are my heroes. . . . Heroes for what they do for us all & what they did for me. They brought my true hero back from war. My dad."[1]

———

In 2011, an installment of the ESPN 30 for 30 documentary series, *The Marinovich Project*, chronicled the rise and fall of former USC and Los Angeles Raiders quarterback Todd Marinovich.[2] The film paints a picture of a burned-out Marinovich—burned out on heroin and pot, and burned out on the pressure of living up to his father Marv's outlandish expectations. There were images and stories of a young boy who was groomed, from the cradle, to be an NFL quarterback. There were images of the pale, skinny, floppy-haired boy being pushed to the absolute limit in the weight room and on the track. Hours and hours were spent throwing the football and then watching video to analyze the thrown football. All with the goal of an NFL career.

Todd Marinovich, at the time in his early forties, spoke into a camera while sitting on the beach—his tired body looking at least fifty, and his wary eyes looking out over the water. Marinovich fills his days now with surfing, art, and music, having left every vestige of the football life behind after one last failed tryout with the Winnipeg Blue Bombers in the CFL; a tryout in which he tore his ACL on the first snap of the first day of practice. "That was fate telling me to get out of the game," said Marinovich.

Marv Marinovich, the father, was largely vilified in the press and in the first half of the piece, looked like the Monster Who Ruined His Son. The elder Marinovich became the poster child for everything bad about the Little League Dad mentality, and Todd was nicknamed "The Robo QB." The Robo QB was groomed to play the position, publicized in local and national media, positioned at the best southern California high school for playing the position, and then ultimately signed by one of college football's glamour programs—the University of Southern California. The Robo QB burned his bridges at USC in favor of partying, and had a short, disappointing NFL career. The family became a very public cautionary tale. Todd equated his father's workout obsessions with his own addictions to drugs.

In the end the two have reunited, with Todd Marinovich getting clean and pursuing a promising career in visual art, and his father, Marv, (also an art major in college) partnering with him on art projects and supporting his son. But what the public doesn't see is that it was Marv at Todd's bedside as he detoxed, cold turkey, from heroin. And what the public also doesn't often see is the humility that comes from hitting personal and professional rock bottoms. This is what is redemptive about films like *The Marinovich Project*.

The Marinovich narrative is interesting in light of the slate of complimentary stories recently published in the *Washington Times* concerning the relationship between Griffin and his father. The Little League Dad appears to be making a bit of a cultural comeback, if the multimillions spent annually on crafting young athletes is any indication. There are strength and conditioning camps, booming private training businesses, college-run camps, websites for college recruitment, and lots of very involved fathers. I witness this firsthand as both a father of young boys and a youth football coach in a suburb where every dad stays for the entire practice, watching along a fence with their arms folded, frowns permanently etched on their faces. My players are fourth graders.

That said, the tone of the *Times* series is curious. It tells of a Robert Griffin childhood spent hurdling on a track, racing up the side of a hill with a tire strapped around his waist, having every *practice* videotaped by mom and then critiqued by dad. Father and son would study videotapes of mobile quarterbacks like Roger Staubach and sprinters like Michael Johnson. And at midnight, after traffic had thinned, they would run a half-mile incline—coined "Griffin Hill"—near their home.[3]

If this were written a certain way, and/or if Robert Griffin were to experience even the slightest of public flake-outs, the articles would lose the aw-shucks, homespun, "Isn't this great!" breathlessness and be replaced by a cynical, "See how little league dads are ruining sports?" sort of tone. The pieces work, largely, because Robert Griffin is working so far. If Todd Marinovich had played in a couple of Pro Bowls and taken the Raiders to a Super Bowl win, we'd be hailing Marv as a genius and shaper of young men. He'd probably be making five figures per appearance on the banquet circuit and have his own book deal.

Wrote *Times* reporter Rich Campbell, "The coach-athlete element of Robert's relationship with his dad fascinates me. I'm reluctant to use the word 'abnormal' because that implies connotations that, frankly, I don't care to apply, but the intensity of their training was extraordinary. . . . I asked myself why Robert Jr.'s strictness, oversight and intensity worked for Robert III when it hasn't worked for so many other father-son relationships. . . . The answer to the question, it turns out, tells us the most important thing about Robert III: He wants to be great. He deeply wants it. His relationship with his dad worked because he *wanted* to be pushed in ways that wouldn't work for many others."[4]

"Now I look back on it and can't believe I did some of that stuff," Griffin III says in the same piece. "If you asked me to do some of that stuff today I probably wouldn't just because of where I am. But the only reason I'm where I am today is because I did that stuff back then. It created my foundation to be the athlete that I am today, whether it's running, [or] jumping."[5]

Robert Griffin III encouraged his parents to move with him to Washington DC after he was drafted by the Redskins, and they rent a townhouse in Gaithersburg, Maryland. Griffin Jr. works a bureaucratic government job, and Griffin's mother, Jackie, touches up his trademark braids every two weeks.

The rising celebrity star of Griffin's parents is indicative of where our culture has come. Allen Iverson's mother—a courtside fixture wearing her son's jersey—made the celebrity NBA mother a mainstream entity. In the *Times*, there are photographs of Griffin's father by his son's side in the ubiquitous NFL draft holding-up-the-jersey photograph, and there are pictures aplenty of the elder Griffins, decked out in jerseys and RG3 gear at FedExField. Bob and Pam Tebow were an integral part of the Tebow public brand, leading up to the draft and even as a part of his NFL career. Family values, as a concept, appears to be making a comeback.

Griffin's parents are savvy enough to know that their über-involvement and unorthodox training methods may be a turnoff to some, and that they have to work to mitigate "Little League Parent" accusations. But the jury on their son is still out. If he becomes the next Steve Young, they'll look like geniuses. If he becomes the next Vince Young (a Rookie of the Year recipient and a subsequent NFL washout, currently unemployed), they'll look . . . well . . . like something else.

"You know how some of the time you have parents who live through their kids?" Jackie Griffin said in the piece. "That wasn't our goal."[6]

As far as I can tell, Griffin worked like an animal and engineered his life so that it would turn out pretty much exactly the way that it's turned out so far. Few people would be willing to put in the work that Griffin put in along the way. He was also, clearly, blessed with an outsized portion of God-given raw talent and has been allowed by God to thus far navigate the puzzle of high school, recruitment, injury, coaching, and other outside factors almost perfectly.

These are the things you already know if you're a Redskins/RG3 follower: He was born in Okinawa, Japan, to army sergeants. The family lived for a time near Tacoma, Washington, and in New Orleans, Louisiana, before settling in Copperas Cove, Texas, which happened to be home to the kind of Texas high school football powerhouse that makes shows like *Friday Night Lights* interesting. I don't know how the Griffins settled in Copperas Cove. The fact is, we now live in a world where parents move their families to make more strategic high school football and recruitment decisions. Gone are the days of a kid growing up in a small town in Indiana, then just playing football for the high school in that small town in Indiana. If the kid has potential, chances are his father finagles a job transfer so that his son can play for the big high school in the well-heeled suburb so as to better his chances for a college scholarship. It's a new era, for better or worse.

The most impressive collection of high school game film I've ever personally viewed belonged to Mississippi legend Marcus Dupree, whose Philadelphia (MS) high school film had a "man amongst boys" quality to it, as the 6-foot-2-inch, 230-pound Dupree ran over, around, and away from high school kids on grainy, black-and-white Super 8 stock. Griffin's Copperas Cove film has a completely different quality. In it, we see Griffin displaying much of the same fluidity and polish we now see on Sunday afternoons. The same smooth drops. The same eyes perpetually upfield, where they're supposed to be. The same slick play-action fakes. The same well-timed, athletic scrambles. We see Griffin doing these things with talented teammates, many of whom went on to college careers, in college-quality high school stadiums. There is a polish and quality to Texas high school football that is indeed unparalleled. Urban Meyer once called it "Grown Man Football." I played small-college football and am convinced that Griffin's high school team would have mopped the field with any college team I was a part of. They looked like grown men.

Perennially ranked in the state standings, Copperas Cove's dedicated football website boasts District Championships in 2004, 2005, 2008, and 2011. It shows big, glossy photos of the school's state-of-the-art football facilities and boasts long lists of players, by graduating class, who went on to play college football. Griffin's graduating class, 2007, was relatively light on college talent, sending only eleven players to the next level, but the 2008 class put twenty-four players on college rosters.[7] The Cove's weight room measures ten thousand square feet, making it roughly three times bigger than that of the Washington Redskins'.

While at Copperas Cove, Griffin was a three-sport star (football, basketball, track). In two seasons as a starting quarterback, Griffin rushed for a total of 2,161 yards and 32 touchdowns while passing for 3,357 yards and 41 touchdowns with 9 interceptions. As a senior, Copperas Cove was 13-2 but lost in the 4A state championship game. In track, Griffin broke state records for the 110-meter and 300-meter hurdles, and as a junior he was named to the *USA Today* All-USA track-and-field team. He also received the Gatorade Boys Texas Track and Field Athlete of the Year Award.

To add to the mythic quality of all this, Griffin was also class president and ranked seventh in his graduating class. Truth be told, it's an experience that few mere mortals can understand, much less relate to.

––––––

For the sake of perspective, consider that before Robert Griffin arrived, Baylor University football hadn't appeared in a bowl game since 1994. They hadn't made a Top 25 rankings appearance since 1986. Baylor's last non-kicker consensus All-American was defensive lineman Santana Dotson in 1991. In 2009, when Griffin was injured in Week 3, they struggled to a 4-8 overall record. It's not much of a stretch, then, to say that Robert Griffin III put Baylor football on the map; and it also goes without saying that carrying the hopes of a program on one's shoulders comes with a great deal of pressure.

I interviewed Michigan high school football legend and former Notre Dame quarterback Evan Sharpley about the pressures that come with being the starting quarterback at a high profile program. Sharpley played quarterback at Notre Dame between megastars Brady Quinn and Jimmy Clausen, and just a few years postgraduation, now eats unnoticed in a Michigan diner as we talk.

"I think the toughest part about playing that position at that level is the potential for letting down your friends and family," he said. "You've got the entire program on your shoulders, and you can't help but think, 'What if I fail? Or what if I don't succeed?' I think with Robert his background prepared him . . . and his commitment to the process each week has allowed him to rise above that. For me, I immersed myself in a lot of different things . . . things that kept me sane. I threw myself into my classroom studies, I got involved with the Fellowship of Christian Athletes, and I fell in love with working out and getting the most out of my body. I really lost myself in those things, and it helped me to deal with the pressure."[8]

A four-star recruit with 4.4 speed and a rocket arm, Griffin was the biggest deal on campus the moment he arrived, much like he was the biggest deal in Washington even before he officially arrived as the team's first-round draft choice. Griffin was being pursued by higher-profile schools like Tennessee, Stanford, Nebraska, and Oregon, where he would have been a perfect choice to pilot Chip Kelly's high-octane offense. He ended up being the perfect player to pilot Art Briles's own high-octane, record-setting offense—brought over from the University of Houston where he coached prior to taking the Baylor job. So why did Griffin choose Baylor? We may never know, but it's clear that he has left an indelible mark on the university.

Griffin arrived at Baylor after graduating high school early, in the spring of 2008. He immediately won a Big 12 track-and-field title in the 400-meter hurdles and, oh yeah, was a semifinalist in hurdles at the 2008 Olympic Trials. Not bad for a college freshman.

As a true freshman, Griffin started and guided the Bears to a 4-8 record, grabbing Big 12 Offensive Freshman of the Year honors. In a 41-21 upset over Texas A&M, the eighteen-year-old Griffin showed the poise and confidence that would mark his tenure at Baylor, throwing for 2 long touchdowns and adding 56 rushing yards. The die had been cast and optimism ran high, but Griffin missed most of the 2009 season, sustaining a torn ACL in the third game of the season. Without him, the team struggled to another disappointing 4-8 record.

Perhaps the most impressive showpieces in Griffin's college career were back-to-back victories over the University of Texas, which has long been the king of college football programs in the state. In 2011, Texas visited Baylor on Senior Day in a game in which the Heisman Trophy may have hung in the balance.

"We thought if we came out with a victory, we could win the Heisman. It's not just about me, it's about all of Baylor Nation," Griffin said. "I don't know if you can say we deserve it, but [it] would definitely be warranted."[9]

Wearing their all-green uniforms, and after a rousing introduction complete with what are now major college football staples—bigger-than-life images of each player on a Jumbotron—Griffin came out and gave a signature performance that sealed Baylor's first 9-win season since 1986. Griffin had to have a big day to cover for a Baylor defense that had already given up 30 or more points eight times in the 2011 season.

On the second play from scrimmage, Griffin eluded the rush, set himself, and threw a deep scoring strike to Kendall Wright, now a member of the Tennessee Titans. They would never look back. Griffin would pass for 320 yards with touchdown strikes of 59 and 39 yards. His first touchdown run, just before the half, gave Baylor the lead; and his second scoring run in the second half salted the game away.

"He's the most dynamic player in the NCAA," said senior running back Terrance Ganaway, who set a Baylor record for rushing yards in a season during the game.[10]

"Not too many years ago, they said Baylor would never be 9-3, would never beat Texas, would never beat Oklahoma," Griffin told the media. "Why not [win the Heisman]?"[11]

It's hard to measure the impact of a win like this on a program like Baylor's. All the major conferences have schools like these—the Baylors, the Purdues, the Northwesterns, the Iowa States—programs that toil in obscurity for years until a signature player or coach arrives to lead them to the Promised Land and a few moments in the sun. Baylor's moment was 2011.

Griffin's final college game, the 2011 Alamo Bowl versus Washington, was the second highest-scoring college bowl game ever and may in many ways captured the spirit of the Griffin era at Baylor. Though he was only average that evening—Griffin was 24-33 for 259 yards and a scoring strike that came on the first drive of the game—the ending was a memorable one for Baylor fans and the perfect note on which to exit the college stage.

ESPN cameras captured Griffin strolling through the bowels of the stadium before the game, wearing the ubiquitous headphones and sunglasses in the building. He already looked the part of the professional. "He's all man," said ESPN analyst Chris Spielman before the game after lauding Griffin's elusiveness and downfield vision.

"This thing truly could go to over 1,000 total yards and over 100 points when it's all said and done," said Spielman of the two high-powered offenses and something-to-be-desired defenses involved. "If so I might take a nosedive off the top of the Alamo Dome," added the legendary linebacker.

"He's a very disciplined person . . . very dedicated," said head coach Art Briles of Griffin on the field before the game. He entered the game with 36 touchdown passes (with only 6 interceptions) and another 9 passes on the ground.

On the first play of the game, Baylor tried a trick play—an inside shovel pass to Kendall Wright that was blown up by Washington. On his second play from scrimmage, Griffin was flushed from the pocket but flicked the ball downfield 25 yards on a rope for a first down. It's the kind of play that makes scouts swoon—escapability, poise, and arm talent all on display in the same play. Later in the series fans got a feel for Griffin's in-pocket mechanics as well. On a third down, he received a shotgun snap, spotted a zone-blitz from the Washington defense, and calmly bounced on his toes until a short receiver came open. Griffin's base was always wide, and his lead foot pointed directly at a receiver on his follow-through. Mechanics like these allowed Griffin to connect on an astonishing 72.4 percent of his passes as a senior. Granted, some of that percentage can be attributed to Art Briles's high-percentage, pass-centric offense; but hitting at that rate in any offense is impressive.

We also saw Griffin connect off play-action, from under center. He got a three-deep zone look from the Washington defense and took an easy 8-yard out. Baylor's no-huddle shotgun pace was blistering, and Washington's defensive line—probably due to a mix of adrenaline and pace—was already standing with hands on hips, and more importantly, standing up and getting pushed around at the line of scrimmage.

The tape also gives one an appreciation for the kinds of hits Griffin has taken as a collegian. He runs the ball and takes shots from Washington's defenders. They're the kind of shots that provide one of the only scouting red flags on Griffin. How long will he last? Every hard shot a ball carrier takes will take a little bit of life out of that player for the long haul and increase the chance of injury.

Baylor takes advantage of Washington's defensive confusion and runs for a first down on a fourth-and-1 play. Immediately following, Griffin hits Kendall Wright for a touchdown. Griffin hit Wright in the flat, and Wright's wiggle and strength took over. "I see perfection out of him," said Spielman of Griffin after the first drive. Following what is, for Baylor, a semileisurely (four-minute) opening drive, the game would turn into a track meet.

Big scoring plays included a 56-yard touchdown run by Washington running back Chris Polk, an 80-yard touchdown catch by Washington's Jermaine Kearse two plays into the second half, and an 89-yard scoring rumble by Baylor's Terrance Ganaway. Kearse struck again, catching and running for 60 yards before getting dragged down, setting up Washington quarterback Keith Price's fourth touchdown toss during the next play.

Ganaway's 43-yard scoring run with just over two minutes remaining sealed the victory for Baylor, and sealed their first 10-win season since 1980. The final scoreboard read Baylor 67, Washington 56. "That was crazy," said Briles, aptly, after the game.

The victory was Baylor's first bowl win since 1992. By that time, Griffin had amassed a truckload of personal accolades, taking home the Davey O'Brien Award, the Manning Award, and the Associated Press Player of the Year Award in addition to the Heisman. He was also an Academic All-American in 2010 and 2011. Griffin finished his college career with an astonishing 78 touchdown passes, against only 17 interceptions. He added another 32 touchdowns on the ground, rushing for over 2,100 yards—even more impressive considering that the NCAA counts sacks against a quarterback's rushing yards.

After the game, Griffin paraded the Alamo Bowl trophy around the field before delivering it to his mother in the first row of the stands, shouting, "We went out in style!" The words were prophetic. Griffin walked off the field to chants of "One more year!" from the Baylor faithful. They could plead, but the handwriting was already on the wall. There wouldn't be another year.

———

A December 2012 feature in *Sports Business Daily* estimated that Griffin's Heisman Trophy was worth an additional $250 million in donations, licensing fees, and ticket sales. Baylor reports a 10 percent increase in giving to the university in the wake of Griffin's success and has plans to break ground on a brand-new, $250-million stadium project.[12]

"It has elevated us on a national level that has never been seen by Baylor University," head coach Art Briles told *Sports Illustrated* when asked about Griffin's impact on the school. "If you ask anybody in the state of Washington or Florida or New York, they're going to know something about Baylor athletics. He's allowed us to have access to every high school student-athlete in America who aspires to play college football at the highest level."[13]

In a study published by ESPN.com in 2007, I analyzed every quarterback drafted in the first round in a fifteen-year period, between 1989 and 2003. I studied them with the hopes of determining how risky it was to draft a signal caller in the first round, and how likely it was that

that player would be a bust. I set the bust metric at 80 games played in the league and a positive touchdown-to-interception ratio. Quarterbacks who won Super Bowls but were unspectacular like Trent Dilfer or who played in Pro Bowls got special consideration as well. The list of first-round busts is long and diverse, and includes such names as Andre Ware, who played in a gimmicky college offense; Dan McGwire, who was 6 feet 8 inches tall; Rick Mirer, who was overhyped in the grand tradition of overhyping Notre Dame quarterbacks; David Klingler, who played in the same gimmicky offense as Ware; and Heath Shuler, Tommy Maddox, and Jim Druckenmiller, just to name a few. For every franchise quarterback like Troy Aikman, there was a Shuler. Even solid starters like Kerry Collins, Donovan McNabb, and Steve McNair (a borderline star) were in seemingly short supply. In all, according to my criteria at least, 53 percent of all quarterbacks drafted in the first round were busts. So why were each of 2012's first-rounders playing at such a high level?

I asked Evan Sharpley why, when historically rookie quarterbacks have struggled, the rookie class of 2012 seemed to be excelling—with Griffin leading the way. "I think the nature of college football has changed in that more programs are utilizing pro-style principles in their offenses," Sharpley said. "A lot of guys are learning more of the Xs and Os in college, so that they're allowed to just step in and play the game of football at the pro level. I also think that in the past pro coaches were staunch about what they wanted to run, whereas now they seem to be throwing the playbook at rookies in chunks rather than all at once."

––––––––

Quarterback guru Terry Shea's résumé includes stints as a quarterback coach with the Kansas City Chiefs, offensive coordinator with the Chicago

Bears, and head coaching at San José State and Rutgers. Of late, he's been in the now-booming business of readying NFL quarterbacking prospects for the draft and NFL scouting combine. Typically, after graduation, quarterbacks will select a guru—others in this cottage industry include former NFL journeymen Steve DeBerg and Chris Weinke—and then spend up to ten weeks with their coaches, working on everything from interviewing skills to on-field decision making. Shea has worked with number one overall picks Sam Bradford and Matthew Stafford, as well as Brady Quinn and Josh Freeman. He worked with Kansas State sensation Collin Klein in the offseason before Klein's final year as a collegian and was, in fact, on the phone with Klein's father when I caught up with him.

"I'm with a player eight or nine hours a day for a ten-week period, so there's the potential for developing a unique relationship with that player," Shea explains. "What I have to offer having been in the NFL is a chance to transfer some of that knowledge to players so that their learning curve can be reduced."[14]

Shea worked with Robert Griffin III at the Athlete's Performance Institute in Arizona and remembers the impression Griffin made as soon as he hit the practice field.

"What grabbed me immediately was his ability to embrace you and make you feel special," he says. "When I walked out onto the practice field, Robert immediately said, 'Hey, Coach, I've been waiting for you—let's get started!' Whether he was greeting an elderly man or an eight-year-old peewee football player, Robert's enthusiasm was infectious."[15]

Because he had worked with so many NFL players, I asked Shea what stood out to him about Griffin and to what we could attribute his early NFL success.

"His coachability was an A+," he says. "Robert can listen with tremendous focus. You can give him a technique in the meeting room or on the chalkboard and he'll immediately capture it physically on the practice field. He doesn't need a lot of repetitions, and he has a skill set that can make those things happen.

"Physically, he reminds me of Matthew Stafford in that he has a quick arm and the ball just jumps out of his hand. With Stafford's skill set, he could really snap at his release point. Robert has the same thing, and that physical attribute speaks highly of what makes one quarterback better than another. Off the field, his humility reminds me of Sam Bradford. They're both Heisman Trophy winners, but that was never mentioned and never brought out with either of them. Leadership-wise, he reminds me of a quarterback I coached in Kansas City named Trent Green who was a special game-day leader. You could see those same things in Robert at his pro day, in the way that he led and directed his teammates. And the fact that the Washington Redskins have named him—a rookie—a team captain is absolutely unprecedented."[16]

There's something very deliberate, positive, and grandfatherly in the way that Shea speaks about his quarterbacks. He has devoted his life and his career to the craft of quarterbacking, and his fingerprints are on the product that is Robert Griffin III. I ask him, in particular, about Griffin's highly developed play-action passing skills.

"That's something we addressed when Robert was with me, and it's one of my signatures as a coach," Shea explains. "I try to make my players magicians with the football, meaning whether they're handing off to a running back or carrying out a fake, everything looks the same. When I watch tape of Robert, I marvel at his ability to make the ball disappear. When we were practicing on the field, I'd critique him to drive for five steps after a handoff and not peek back at the ball. There is nothing lazy about Robert's game, and if the Redskins demand it, he'll do it."[17]

I suggest to Shea that Griffin's supreme confidence and athletic ability enable him to have such confidence in his play-action game. But regarding athleticism, there is the dubious record of running quarterbacks burning out early and failing to win titles.

"My biggest question is whether the quarterback is a passer first and a runner second," Shea says. "You win with your arm, but you keep games alive with your legs. When Steve Young developed his skill, he was a passer first and a runner second. That way you have a longer shelf life and greater potential to be productive in the league. Robert is an innately strong athlete and has a tremendously strong frame that should keep him healthy, provided he commits to being a passer first."[18]

Shea suggests that the proclivity toward passing in today's college programs results in passers who are more ready to step in and succeed at the pro level.

"I once asked Robert how many balls he threw in a typical practice at Baylor, and he said 150–175. That's a lot of throws. I really believe that college quarterbacks come out having thrown so many more passes in competitive situations than their predecessors in past eras. Many of these colleges are pass-first offenses in the Bill Walsh style. They use the pass to set up the run. Some of these guys throw the ball 55 times a game, and they're making *different* kinds of throws. They're touching the ball, driving the ball, and they're probably throwing 200 to 300 more passes in their careers in game situations than the guys who came out a decade ago. When you take bright, intelligent quarterbacks like Sam Bradford and Robert Griffin, and combine it with those reps . . . you're going to get a pretty polished product.

"But there's a ceiling to how much you can study tape and how much you can practice. There's an innate quality that the great quarterbacks have. I believe it comes down to vision, and the great ones see in three dimensions. With Trent Green, it was almost like he saw things in slow motion. He'd come off the field during a game and tell me what he saw, and then when I'd sit down to watch the film on Monday morning, it was exactly what he saw in game speed. He was amazing. I'd say, 'Man, how did you see that?' Robert is the same way."[19]

2

FROM BOBBY DOUGLASS TO TIMOTHY TEBOW TO RG3: A BRIEF HISTORY OF RUNNING QUARTERBACKS

Whenever I write about the past, which I do often, I make a trip to downtown East Lansing and the Curious Book Shop, which is the kind of place that has everything, book-wise, including a clerk who looks like Moby and can make you feel stupid for not having an MFA in poetry. He does this on a subconscious (for him) level, and I've actually gotten to where I kind of like it in a weird way. Anyway, you have to ask Moby to let you upstairs, which is where they keep the Midwest's most exhaustive archive of old football books and magazines. The upstairs at Curious is like the best kind of museum. It's a walk back in football history where for a few bucks I can walk out with a retro football magazine or paperback that they slide into an old-school paper bag.

Today I'm searching for running-quarterback-related ephemera, and I'm searching for an answer to a question that will provide some backbone for a narrative about a kid who is taking the NFL by storm and who will either revolutionize the league and Madison Avenue (if some writers are to be believed) or get his body beat up, never play in a Super Bowl, and never really live up to expectations (if others are to be believed).

My question is, simply stated: Is being a disappointment the fate of all running quarterbacks in the NFL?

There's a wanton disregard for the future in Robert Griffin's style of play. It suggests invincibility. Griffin, with his mad dashes and headfirst dives, thinks he'll be doing this forever. We know he's wrong. We know that the brilliance he's creating today will rob him of his football tomorrows, which is part of what makes the todays so interesting. If we knew he could do this for a decade, we wouldn't appreciate it as much.

IT ALL STARTED WITH BOBBY DOUGLASS

In 1972, Chicago Bears quarterback Bobby Douglass averaged 6.2 yards per carry, setting an NFL single-season rushing record for quarterbacks, with 968 yards.[1] In a 16-game season, he would have topped 1,000 yards easily. Douglass was a second-round draft choice out of Kansas, where he was an All-American. He never quite panned out with Chicago, however, and is most famous for taping crude lists of play calls to a piece of cardboard on his wrist so that he could remember them in the huddle.

Douglass, of course, was a sensational athlete. He looked the part of the pro quarterback at 6 feet 4 inches tall and 225 pounds. Lantern jaw. Big arm. Rawboned. Could throw the ball nearly the length of the field on the fly. Unfortunately, Douglass had trouble hitting any of the Chicago receivers with it, as his career passer rating of 48.5 is astonishingly low for someone who played that many years (eleven) in the league. Douglass completed over 50 percent of his passes in only one season (1977, his second to last), and that was a season in which he attempted only 31 passes. He threw 4 touchdown passes against the Buffalo Bills at the beginning of his career in 1970, but essentially had a downhill trajectory thereafter. He goes down in Bear history with Virgil Carter, Jack Concannon, Gary Huff, Greg Landry, and Bob Avellini in a series of forgettable Bear quarterbacks who held the position between Billy Wade and Jim McMahon. In his defense, Douglass played exclusively for horrible teams—the early-'70s Bears, mid-'70s Saints, and 1979 Packers were all horrendous—for the duration of his career, which begs the question: Were they bad *because* Douglass never learned to pass, or did Douglass never learn to pass because he was always running for his life?

Which begs the other question: Do running quarterbacks experience limited passing success *because of* their prodigious athletic ability? Is it easier to keep running than to learn to pass in the NFL? Douglass played eleven years in the league, which is nothing to sneeze at, but he never came close to touching the promise he showed as a college player at Kansas. Perhaps he was too enamored with the run, or perhaps when pass protection broke down, as it often did on those dreadful Bears teams, it was easier to let athletic ability take over than to learn to read the whole field.

Caveat: You're probably wondering how I can leave Fran Tarkenton, who played in—and lost—four Super Bowls out of this meditation. Tarkenton was a scrambler, not a runner. There's a difference. Tarkenton scrambled to create space and time to pass. Douglass, Vick, RG3, Newton, Tebow, et al., run to gain yards, and after they pass the line of scrimmage essentially become running backs.

THE MICHAEL VICK PROJECT

Philadelphia Eagles quarterback Mike Vick experienced an unprecedented level of hype when he left Virginia Tech as a redshirt sophomore. Vick ran a jaw-dropping 4.33-second 40-yard dash at his Pro Day (he supposedly ran 4.26 as a freshman), leaving scouts drooling at his athletic potential. Vick was also the owner of a 38-inch vertical jump and a 515-pound squat. Explosive. But compared to Griffin's, Vick's college statistics were downright pedestrian. In 2000, Vick threw 9 touchdown passes (7 INTs) with an extremely average completion percentage of 54 percent. His real impact came on the ground, however, where he rushed for over 600 yards and 9 touchdowns.

In many ways, Vick was the object of media fascination, and that fascination led to his ascension up the draft boards. Vick was the subject of cover stories in both *Sports Illustrated* and *ESPN The Magazine,* chronicling his rise from the public housing projects of Newport News, Virginia.

Said his cousin, NFL quarterback Aaron Brooks, in the *ESPN* piece, "If he tries to get cute and run around all over the place with the ball like he did in college, the guys in the NFL will knock his butt out."[2] Largely, Brooks's words proved to be prophetic, as Vick has been the victim of his own courage and running talent. Like Bobby Douglass before him (1972), he's started all 16 games only once (2006) in his career and has played in zero Super Bowls. There is talk of the Eagles replacing him with 2012 draft choice Nick Foles, who is a Vick foil in every way—tall, white, and immobile. It seems that excitement has nearly gone out of fashion in Philadelphia.

The *ESPN* piece ended breathlessly, stating, "The NFL has never seen a physical package like this before and no one in this league—no one—wants to be tattooed with the most vile phrase of all: I passed on Michael Vick."[3]

In reality, Vick's "physical package" seemed more suited to running back, where it's no liability to being short (he's only 6 feet tall) and fearless. By comparison, Griffin has benefited from a body more suited to the position (he's 6 feet 2 inches and 223 pounds), and a college offense that was much more sophisticated and pass-centric than the one Vick piloted at Virginia Tech in the late 1990s.

Most of a career and a dog-fighting conviction later, it seems likely that there are probably a good number of personnel guys who are glad they passed on Vick. His career passer rating of 80.7 puts him in the neighborhood of Jeff Hostetler (who started a Super Bowl with the Giants), Damon Huard (forgettable), Jeff George (disappointing), and Warren Moon (great but no Super Bowls). For what it's worth, both Dan Fouts and John Elway rank lower, proving that passer rating isn't everything. For what it's worth (again), Vick has played in four Pro Bowls, but the Pro Bowl has become sort of a joke as it seems to be an annual February tradition for players to try like crazy to get out of playing in it.

Vick is currently holding on to his starting job in Philadelphia by a very thin thread. He's lost several starting offensive linemen and seems to be running for his life in each and every start, having been sacked 27 times and knocked down 83 times after Week 9. Vick has fumbled the ball 10 times to go with 9 interceptions and appears destined to lose his job to traditional pocket passer Nick Foles.

In a Week 10 matchup with rival Dallas at home, Vick and Andy Reid both seem to be playing for their jobs. An Eagles loss seems to suggest that the season is over, and the club begins planning and playing for 2013—which means, first and foremost, firing Andy Reid and finding a replacement for Vick.

After throwing a TD pass to Riley Cooper in the first quarter, Vick is hit hard on successive plays in the second. He's pile-driven into the ground by Jay Ratliff, then hit on a delayed blitz by linebacker Ernie Sims, sending him to the bench for the rest of the afternoon with a concussion. Foles, his replacement, is mostly solid, going 22-32 for 219 yards, a touchdown, and a pick. What's lost in the Eagles' post-loss rhetoric is that Vick was pretty efficient with 6-9 for 70 yards and a score before leaving the game with a concussion. A concussion that could end his run as a starter in Philadelphia.

PASTOR RANDALL CUNNINGHAM

Former Eagles (and Vikings) quarterback Randall Cunningham was a lot like Robert Griffin III. Both sensational athletes. Both somewhat slight-looking and long of limb. Both capable of making the kinds of plays that end up on highlight reels. Both doing it with smiles on their faces, at least initially for Cunningham, and a modicum of joy that is lacking in the modern NFL. Cunningham, like Griffin, seemed to enjoy his job. For a while his ceiling seemed limitless, both on and off the field.

"When I first saw Randall Cunningham at our first minicamp together I thought he'd be the greatest quarterback to ever play the position," said then-incumbent Eagles quarterback Ron Jaworski on the NFL Network examination of the top mobile quarterbacks. "He had that kind of talent."[4]

The younger brother of legendary USC Trojan and later New England Patriot running back Sam "The Bam" Cunningham, Randall was being recruited as a defensive back by USC, but chose instead to attend the University of Nevada, Las Vegas, where he would be able to play quarterback. He enrolled at UNLV in 1981, where his brother Bruce was a defensive back. To be an athletic black quarterback in the early 1980s was to have limited options, as it seemed coaches only saw a future wide receiver or defensive back.

His decision paid off, as Cunningham won the starting job in the second game of his sophomore season, and over the next three years became only the third quarterback in NCAA history (with John Elway and Doug Flutie) to throw for 2,500 yards in three consecutive seasons. Like RG3 (and unlike Vick and Bobby Douglass) he had a considerable body of work as a collegiate passer—enough that the Eagles made him their second pick in the 1985 draft.

"Randall Cunningham—he was one of the first supreme athletes to play that [quarterback] position," said Jon Gruden in an *E:60* special on Cunningham. "I was an enigma to people back then," said Cunningham on the special. "And yes, I did hang out with, you know, people like Johnny Gill from New Edition and Arsenio Hall . . . that star status, it almost grabbed me."[5]

Richard Glazer wrote in a 1990 *Football Digest* feature, "I think Randall will be pro football's answer to Michael Jordan." "Randall's potential in this [marketing] area is enormous," said agent Jim Steiner in the same piece. "He is 26, and he's already one of the most visible and exciting players in the league."[6]

"He is doing commercials. He is selling his face on posters and t-shirts. He is hosting TV and radio shows. He is doubling his fee for a personal appearance, and he is just scratching the surface," gushed Glazer in the *Football Digest* piece. Cunningham, like Griffin, seized the moment when he had the opportunity, but he largely found that moment to be unsatisfying and—as all moments by definition are—temporary.

By 1995, Randall Cunningham was a backup. "I became a prideful person," he said on the *E:60* special. "Why was that a bad thing?" asked the interviewer.

"Pride always comes before the fall," replied Cunningham, who left the game for an entire season (1996) before returning to the field with the Minnesota Vikings. During his year off, he started a granite countertop business in Las Vegas, where he played his college ball at UNLV. Cunningham explains that people questioned his motives, saying, "Randall Cunningham wouldn't do this. He wouldn't be on the floor, dirty and scraping the floor." But, as Cunningham explains, "[God] was allowing me to humble myself under His mighty hand."

He piloted a record-setting offense in Minnesota with a young Randy Moss and came to within a last-second, Morten Andersen field goal of playing in his first Super Bowl. He would never get that close again.

Cunningham's best season came in 1990 when he threw for 30 touchdowns (against 13 picks) and added another 934 yards on the ground. He was Bobby Douglass and Vick-esque in terms of rushing output, but he showed poise and polish in the pocket as well. By age thirty-five, he was a Minnesota Viking and had curtailed his running exploits (down to 134 yards), but threw for 34 TDs against only 10 INTs. The presence of two Hall of Fame–level receivers in Cris Carter (who should be in) and Randy Moss (who will be in) couldn't have hurt.

Cunningham was a Pro Bowler four times and a first-team All-Pro selection once. He also played in zero Super Bowls.

KORDELL STEWART

The Pittsburgh Steelers made Kordell Stewart the twenty-eighth pick of the second round in the 1995 NFL Draft. He joined a team that had Neal O'Donnell installed as the starting quarterback. Though O'Donnell won a Super Bowl, he goes down (along with Trent Dilfer) as the kind of Super Bowl–winning quarterback teams were always trying to upgrade. Hence, the Stewart selection.

Stewart made his name at Colorado at a time when colleges were still running old-school option offenses, preventing athletic quarterbacks like Stewart from really blossoming as defense-reading pocket passers. He finished his career with 77 TDs and 84 INTs. His best season, passing and rushing, was in 2001 when he played in a Pro Bowl, but Stewart is probably best known for his unique contributions as a running back/receiver/package quarterback in 1995. The Steelers never fully committed to Stewart as a quarterback, eventually replacing him with Tommy Maddox.

WHAT HAPPENED TO VINCE YOUNG?

As of this writing, Vince Young has been out of professional football for nearly three months. He was signed to a one-year contract with the Buffalo Bills before the 2012 season and was subsequently released after being beaten out by journeymen Tyler Thigpen, of Coastal Carolina University, and Ryan Fitzpatrick, who played his college ball at Harvard. This after a surreal and disappointing season as Michael Vick's backup in Philadelphia, where there may have been as much dysfunction in the quarterback room (Vick and Young together) as there has ever been on one NFL team at any particular time.

Another surreality is that one can still visit VinceYoung.com, buy a pair of Vince Young–inspired Reebok trainers, download a Vince Young screen saver, and make a donation to the Vince Young Foundation, even though Young is unemployed, recently filed for bankruptcy, and is embroiled in lawsuits with former agents and financial advisers. It comes down to this: Young is alleged to have spent most of his $26 million guaranteed signing bonus. And after a bizarre flake-out in Tennessee, he became something of a pariah in NFL circles—even though his numbers aren't that bad, and even though relative ham-and-eggers like Rex Grossman, Brady Quinn, Bruce Gradkowski, Tarvaris Jackson, and (gasp) Curtis Painter are still drawing NFL paychecks as of this writing.

Vince Young was 6 feet 5 inches, 230 pounds, and ran in the 4.5s at the NFL Scouting Combine. He had a sensational end to an already sensational college career by lighting up USC in the Rose Bowl—killing them with both his feet and his arm. It was a performance that could make an NFL owner susceptible to the kind of "I want him no matter what it means for our team" sentiment that so often happens with media sensations who may or may not fit the NFL mold (see: Flutie, Doug). That susceptibility led to Tennessee owner Bud Adams acquiring Young, and then to Young's hot start and subsequent personal and professional free fall in Tennessee.

To be frank, the most significant knock on Vince Young coming out of Texas was that Vince Young was unintelligent. To be fair, that was the knock on Terry Bradshaw and Dan Marino as well; and both of them ended up in the Hall of Fame, proving that there's a certain kind of intelligence required of an NFL quarterback, but it's not necessarily the kind of intelligence that figures equations or writes papers on Proust. Plenty of guys who were unintelligent (at least according to the Wonderlic Cognitive Ability Test) found ways to flourish in the NFL, even at the NFL's most intellectually taxing position.

The early book on Young was *All He Did Was Win* (which is also the book on Tebow, depending on who you ask); *All He Did Was Win* being another way to say, "His statistics are pretty ordinary (in Tebow's case even bad), and he hasn't really even played that well, but we're still winning games and exciting the fan base." Here's a short but impressive list of what Young managed to accomplish in his first few seasons:

- 2006 NFL Rookie of the Week Awards (four separate weekly awards)
- 2006 NFL AP Offensive Rookie of the Year
- 2006 Diet Pepsi NFL Rookie of the Year
- 2007 Pro Bowl
- 2008 EA Sports Madden Football Cover
- 2010 Pro Bowl

What Young appeared to lack was emotional intelligence. He struggled to communicate clearly in the interview room and was overly emotional on and off the field. He was playing for a player's coach (Jeff Fisher), in a relatively laid-back media market (Nashville), in the kind of place where, in player/management conflicts, people were almost always going to side with management. Simply stated, all Vince Young really needed to do to please the Nashville fan base was to exhibit a little bit of thankfulness for his opportunity and the kind of professionalism that shows a commitment to steady improvement. He exhibited neither.

Young may have found it difficult to follow in the footsteps of former Titans legend Steve McNair. McNair had won the undying loyalty of the fan base with his gritty, steady play and mature leadership. The end of the line in Tennessee for Young came after a 2010 loss to Washington when Young threw his pads into the stands, then stormed out of the locker room after an altercation with Fisher. His days as a Titan were over.

Young's final significant pro action, in a Week 13 start for Philadelphia in relief of an injured Mike Vick in 2011, was a microcosm of his time in the league—and really of the entire disappointing Philly squad (4-7), whom Young himself awkwardly anointed a "Dream Team" after his signing. It was cold and loud in Seattle, and across the field the Seahawks were starting their own imminently forgettable (but still employed) quarterback, Tarvaris Jackson.

Young's very first play from scrimmage was an interception on a deep floater into double coverage—the kind of play that a savvy high school quarterback knows how to avoid. Flushed from the pocket and showing his trademark athleticism, Young should have thrown the ball into the stands or slid for whatever positive yardage he could manage. Instead, he threw up a head-scratcher of a pick. Young—and indeed the entire team—looked cold and apathetic on the sideline as the booth reviewed the pick.

DeSean Jackson's lazy routes and Young's questionable decisions explained the season and encapsulated Andy Reid's frustrating tenure leading ultratalented, underachieving, and at times mentally absent Eagles teams.

It could and should be argued that the third-quarter interception, intended for Riley Cooper with the Eagles down 24-7, wasn't Young's fault. He stood tall in the face of a heavy rush and fired an accurate strike over the middle to Cooper, who let the ball bounce off his hands and right to a waiting Seahawks defender. His third and fourth picks, however, were both unconscionable.

Displaying lackadaisical game management with the Eagles still in it at 24-14, Young lazily walked his team to the line and locked in on running back LeSean McCoy, running a flare into the left flat. Seahawk linebacker Michael Hawthorne, an undrafted free agent from TCU, jumped the route, plucked the ball out of the air, and raced untouched the other way for a touchdown. Later, Young would throw another soft deep ball into double coverage for his fourth and final interception.

He would be photographed on the sideline with his head in his hands, kneeling, either in a posture of prayer or deep discouragement. Either way, the interception was his last significant NFL play.

TEBOW

At the end of the 2011 NFL season, the New York Giants walked off the field in Indianapolis hoisting the Vince Lombardi trophy awarded to the last team standing. A paragon of good management and consistency, the Giants have been a model NFL franchise. Their New York–area counterparts, the Jets, haven't appeared in a Super Bowl since Joe Namath famously guaranteed victory in Super Bowl III. It could be argued that Namath was the team's last marquee quarterback, and that the intervening years have been marked by bad coaching (remember Rich Kotite, Lou Holtz, Bruce Coslet, and a pre-USC-dynasty Pete Carroll?), bad drafting (Blair Thomas, Browning Nagle, et al.), and poor play. Off the field, the Jets have competed for newspaper space with the Giants, Knicks, Yankees, and Mets, often creating an intriguing story-behind-the-story. Into this story strides the most public evangelical in, perhaps, the history of public evangelicals—Jesus and Billy Graham notwithstanding.

Jets owner Woody Johnson seemed to be an ideological fit for Tebow. The problem is, Johnson's football team really didn't need him, and with the exception of Jacksonville, no one else in the league wanted him.

Known for the Heisman Trophy and trademarking prayer in the end zone, Timothy Richard Tebow, he of the lantern jaw and evangelical hero star profile, made his living running and throwing the football in Florida's spread-option offense and has struggled to find a place in the pro game thus far. Given his relative inexperience under center, his looping, unorthodox throwing motion, and his accuracy issues, Tebow hasn't been given much of an opportunity to roll as a full-time quarterback for either the Denver Broncos or the New York Jets. When he got a chance to start for Denver in 2011, he made the most of his opportunity in the win column (arguably the only column that matters) but was still statistically forgettable; and he was ultimately expendable, even given his rabid Denver-area evangelical fan base, when Peyton Manning became available.

Tebow's last 3 regular-season starts for the Broncos, all losses, were all dreadful performances statistically, culminating in a 6 for 22 (27 percent) with an interception outing against Kansas City. This is the Tebow stat line that keeps coordinators up at night, and ultimately keeps teams from going "all in" on Tebow, despite his proven ability to stay on television and sell merchandise.

As of this writing, he's only attempted two passes as a New York Jet and is sitting behind an underperforming Mark Sanchez on the depth chart.

"The Jets trade was solely to put fans in the seats and generate interest," said one New York–based sports agent when I asked him about New Yorkers' perspectives on the quarterback. "That move was designed to sell, and I was afraid it would adversely affect Mark Sanchez's confidence . . . and it has. His confidence is shot. They've put in a few packages for him, and they haven't worked. You look at his [Tebow's] lack of accuracy and his elongated throwing motion, and he is not an NFL quarterback. He's not the answer."[7]

Tebow probably most closely resembles Douglass, as they're both big, physical, and white. They were running quarterbacks who were as likely to run you over as run around you. They're also both dreadfully inaccurate in the pass game. Tebow's biggest contribution has come off the field, where he is arguably the most saleable (and polarizing) star to come along in the last decade being that he is clean-cut, articulate, and clean-living.

He's the kind of quarterback who, in year three of his career, columnists are having to basically write "position papers" about. You're either a Tebow apologist or a Tebow hater as a columnist, and people like Stephen A. Smith and Skip Bayless are making careers out of being at the opposite ends of the Tebow spectrum. A network (ESPN) so adamantly opposed to anything smacking of social conservatism or Christianity is also adept at knowing where its financial bread is buttered, airing hour after hour of Tebow updates and Tebow documentaries. Tebow, quite simply, is selling better than he's playing, and his supporters don't seem to care.

SO WHAT DOES THIS MEAN FOR RG3?

What all of these quarterbacks have in common is that for a time they all excited their respective fan bases with their electrifying play and athletic potential. Carolina's Cam Newton, who has done the same thing so far, will be discussed at length in a later chapter. Even today, the "running quarterback" debate rages, with headlines like "Running Quarterbacks Revolutionizing Game, but Not Ready to Win It All Yet" (CBS Sports, by former NFL scout Pat Kirwan) and the more strident, "Running Quarterbacks Do Not Win Super Bowls" from Edwin Torres at Yahoo! Sports.

"When you look at the other quarterbacks who make running with the ball a big part of what they do, the wins don't necessarily follow the rushing yardage," Kirwan writes. "In fact, the top four rushing quarterbacks since 2006, excluding Rodgers, have five winning seasons out of 19."[8]

I asked Hall of Fame quarterback Jim Kelly, a friend, if he thought a team could win a title with a runner at quarterback. Before I could even finish the question, he said, "No." When asked to elaborate, he explained, "Running quarterbacks can't make it though a whole season, for one. Also, you need a quarterback who understands how to read defenses."[9]

In a sense, Griffin enters the league as a more polished passer than all the players listed above. Griffin attempted 1,159 passes as a collegiate player, far eclipsing Vick's college passing experience, and, though some of it is attributed to his team's offense, his completion percentage was an exceptional 66 percent. By comparison, Vince Young attempted only 718 passes at Texas, and Vick attempted an astonishingly low 332 passes at Virginia Tech, completing only 56 percent of them. Griffin was his high school's class president, graduating seventh in his class, and graduated from Baylor with a 3.67 GPA, proving that intelligence, maturity, and the ability to learn shouldn't be an issue.

In a pre-draft scouting report, *Pro Football Weekly* summarized Griffin's vast upside, saying of Griffin,

> Outstanding deep-ball touch and accuracy; can drop it in a bucket and place it in tight spots. Highly competitive. Can adjust his throwing platform on the move, hasten his delivery and snap it from multiple arm angles. Can uncork it with ease. Quick to locate open receivers and will keep his eyes downfield in the face of duress. Competitive with the ball in his hands and picks up yardage in chunks. Has sprinter's straightline speed and is effective scrambling outside the pocket. Comes from a

military family that has instilled structure in his life. Extremely smart. Mentally tough—responds to a challenge. Came through in the clutch against Oklahoma and Washington and showed he can produce under the bright lights. Rare production. Gained a staggering 10.7 yards per attempt and proved capable of consistently flipping the field in a few plays.[10]

As important, he was the unquestioned locker-room leader at Baylor and seems to have quickly adopted the same role with the Washington Redskins.

"Robert has been the same every Monday," Redskins offensive coordinator Kyle Shanahan told CBSSports.com. "Whether he's been good or bad, whether we've won or lost, he comes in upbeat and eager to get better. He comes in wanting to know what he did bad. He enjoys football. He enjoys the guys. He's fun to be around."[11]

"There are a lot of different ways we measure quarterbacks on and off the field," said former NFL head coach and current NFL Network analyst Steve Mariucci in the *Washington Post*. "This guy seems to have an 'A' grade in all of them."[12]

As a pro, Griffin will need to make more of a commitment to the passing game than Douglass and Vick, be less of a sideshow attraction than Tebow, and show more off-the-field maturity under fire than Vince Young. The film would suggest that for modern-era role models, he should look to Cunningham, who—though a highlight reel waiting to happen as a young player—developed into a polished passer and almost a Super Bowl quarterback late in his career.

3

PRO DAY AND THE INEXACT
SCIENCE OF NFL SCOUTING

After so many years, and so many trips, these college football practice facilities all begin to look the same. They all have the same brushed steel and wood interiors—masculine and calibrated to intimidate and impress. The same security keypad. The same heavy glass doors. The same more-attractive-than-necessary receptionist. The same impressive photos and jerseys of players from Good Old State U who have gone on to live their dreams in the NFL. The same trophies. The same banners boasting program achievements.

For one day each year, these facilities play host to a very select group of NFL guests—scouts, coaches, and general managers who descend upon the place and commence watching film, interviewing coaches and trainers, and trying, ultimately, to take the risk out of what is at its essence an extremely risky endeavor on which teams lose untold millions of dollars each year (see: Leaf, Ryan, and countless others). For an NFL club, spending millions on volatile college kids in the NFL draft is bad business, but it's the kind of bad business that teams need to become reasonably good at. Hence, Pro Days, hosted on campus, in which scouts can get a look at every draftable player from a given school.

A few years ago I secured an invite to Central Michigan's Pro Day, the year that they had a surprise first-round draft choice named Joe Staley, whose pro-day workout literally changed his life.

The scouts began arriving before dawn. Being that it was Michigan in the spring, it still felt like winter, as there was a chill in the air and a heavy frost on the ground. The Oldsmobile Aleros and Kia Spectras pulled up past the empty concrete bowl of Kelly-Shorts Stadium and, one by one, bleary-eyed serious-looking men emerged, all stamped and affiliated in officially licensed team gear. They weren't so much individuals as symbols of the teams they represented, and the men they were there to watch weren't so much individuals as they were collections of numbers—heights, weights, vertical jumps, bench reps, and 40-yard-dash times. Dehumanization, it seemed, was in the air.

Their process would be similar, regardless of team. They would have access to private rooms for viewing Central Michigan's film, as well as specific film cut-ups of each player in whom they had an interest. They would receive access to the training room, where they would be able to speak to team trainers about any lingering injury issues, or simply ask the trainer if said player was a decent guy. Often these off-the-beaten-path interviews reveal a great deal more about the athlete than did talking to the athlete himself—schooled as he is in the manly art of talking a lot while revealing nothing. "Does he play through pain? How does he treat people in the program?" These are the questions that can reveal the actual substance of a man's character.

Oddly enough, that day's events would be formative for a number of the men involved. Central Michigan's head coach during the 2006 season was Brian Kelly, who shortly afterward accepted a head coaching job at the University of Cincinnati. He's currently the head coach at Notre Dame, where he took his overachieving squad to a BCS Title Game in 2012.

Another man with a lot on the line—in fact, the man I was there to write about—was defensive end Dan Bazuin. A quiet, genuinely humble (which is saying something), gentle-giant, Bazuin hailed from the tiny town of McBain, where his parents were farmers. He projected as a classic overachiever who got the most out of his 6-foot-3-inch, 272-pound frame and used it to set school and Mid-American Conference records for sacks. Bazuin didn't like to talk. He wasn't gregarious. He didn't walk around like he owned the place. He didn't have that detached strut that most elite athletes have perfected. He also didn't fake being humble, which in my imperfect opinion is way more aggravating than actual arrogance. These are all reasons I rooted heavily for him that day. He was a good kid who, again in my imperfect opinion, deserved whatever good came his way.

After film viewing and training room visits, the scouts were herded to Central's large weight room, featuring 7,100 square feet of state-of-the-art training gear. Here, players are officially weighed and measured, so that their program height and weight (traditionally overinflated) can be tested against reality.

"When I came to CMU, I was 215 pounds and played tight end," said Staley in the team's official media guide. "Since coach Longo (strength coach) came, I've put on almost 80 pounds but haven't lost any of my speed. I may be an offensive lineman, but I can still run like a tight end. Our training is specific for each position, so that what we do will carry over onto the field."[1]

Like Griffin's alma mater, Central Michigan was an example of the kind of program that constantly did battle against marquee football-factory brethren for respect, coveted television slots, and recruiting talent. Subsequently they could often be seen in off-peak time slots on the ESPN family of networks. There were lots of Tuesday and Thursday night games to work around, but for Kelly, the tradeoff was worth it.

"Our goal heading into year three of this program was to increase exposure at the national level, and with this schedule and these television opportunities, we have certainly done that," he said.[2] It was that exposure, and that success, that Kelly would parlay into a job just one rung higher on the ever-changing coaching food chain.

In the weight room, as each player was weighed and measured, it was oddly quiet. It's customary in weight rooms for rap or heavy metal music to be throbbing. That morning, there was nothing but the sound of a player's name being called, and that player stepping to a platform to have his arms, hands, and entire body measured, and then be placed atop a scale. Often the player would remove headphones, stand for the measurements, and then put the headphones right back on. Their nerves were palpable. For the scouts, the events took on an air of grim resignation, as if they all realized how unusual it was to travel around the country, en masse, in this fashion, to weigh and measure college kids, but if one of them decided to stay home, that would be the day in which something amazing was discovered.

Bazuin measured a shade under 6 feet 4 inches tall—a little short by NFL defensive line standards. Staley measured over 6 feet 5 inches tall and just a few scant years ago was setting high school records in track, where he was a 200-meter-dash specialist.

After measurements, players began to slide beneath a bar weighted with 225 pounds—two "big plates" on each side of the bar. For most of these athletes, 225 is child's play, but it's a standard NFL metric just because football is a game with (unlike baseball) so few standard metrics that translate to on-field performance. As Bazuin slid under the bar and began to churn out reps, the rest of the room was stationary, save for a large group of men in NFL gear hovering over the bar and writing notes. Somebody, somewhere, shouted "let's go Danny!" He racked the bar loudly and the next man up slid in.

Even at Central, there was a hierarchy. The players—like Bazuin, Staley, and center Drew Mormino—who had been fortunate enough to be invited to the NFL Combine, wore their Combine sweatshirts like badges of honor. They had the advantage (or disadvantage?) of having been evaluated like this before. Their sweatshirts bore NFL-assigned serial numbers such as OL 419. The others, like seniors Doug Kress and Mike Ogle, stood like cattle . . . hoping . . . praying, for a glance or word of encouragement from an NFL scout . . . anything from anyone who could validate their dream. If only they, too, could be a number.

———

Robert Griffin III made a statement by refusing to submit himself to a private workout with the Indianapolis Colts, owners of the number one overall pick in the NFL draft. Part of being an elite prospect means that a player can retain, and sometimes even exert, his individuality. Colts owner Jim Irsay insisted via his Twitter feed that the club hadn't made up its mind about Andrew Luck, which may or may not have been true.

"The decision by Griffin and his agent—CAA's Ben Dogra—should be praised," wrote NFL.com columnist Ian Rapoport. "Griffin's refusal to be used by teams to create leverage against other prospects, perhaps for contractual reasons, should be celebrated. In addition, Redskins fans finally found a player who is simply dying to be the face of their franchise."[3] For his part, Dogra said in the NFL.com piece: "In pretty much every case, it makes no sense . . . But in this one, it ends all speculation. This kid is legit. No need to waste his time or the franchise's time."[4]

It is, no doubt, a bold and different move by Griffin. It could be understood in one of several ways. One, Griffin was convinced that Indianapolis was taking Luck, and was just doing due diligence or trying to exercise negotiating leverage by working him out. Or perhaps Griffin was non-verbally stating his desire to come to Washington and be the face of their franchise. It's not quite the same as LeBron compiling an All-Star team with the Miami Heat, but it is another example of an athlete with leverage using it to his full advantage. Typically, in the NFL draft process, an athlete is at the mercy of the system and must go and play where he is drafted. Few—like Bo Jackson or John Elway—have dared to manipulate the system to their own ends and been successful. The move proves that Griffin has moxie, and has an ironclad belief in his own abilities.

Griffin's only public display of arm talent—he didn't throw at the combine—is at his Pro Day. Blue-chip prospects will often host their own Pro Days, but Griffin instead opts to participate in Baylor's event, doing only the throwing drills.

Though historically private affairs, ESPN has taken to covering the higher-profile Pro Days, and this one certainly qualifies.[5] As is typical for him, Griffin is portrayed as relaxed and completely in command of his surroundings. He wears an Adidas shirt already emblazoned with one of his catchphrases, "No Pressure, No Diamonds." He is about the business of building a brand identity before even taking an NFL snap.

One of Griffin's greatest strengths is that he always seems happy and confident. He moves about the Pro Day with a sort of half-grin on his face—the grin that people often wear when they know something juicy or intriguing that the rest of the room doesn't. Since his sensational season and his Heisman, he already moves like a person who is used to having rooms full of people looking at him and talking about him. He seems neither put off nor especially stressed out by this reality. On the contrary, he seems to thrive on it.

And what's interesting from a leadership standpoint is that his teammates don't appear to resent him for the attention he's receiving. Like many great leaders, Griffin leads, primarily, by being awesome at what he does and enabling others to do things like win, get drafted, and get paid. Other Baylor prospects clearly benefited from the national spotlight's glare on their quarterback. This, of course, makes it much easier to lead in other ways, as does his legendary work ethic. If nothing else, Griffin's teammates see that he's willing to put in as much or more work as they do, making his stardom not only tolerable but welcome. What's unique about Griffin is that he seems equally adept at leading with his words and his actions.

He leads his receivers through a warm-up, and in doing so works with Baylor's center to show the scouts in attendance that he's comfortable taking a snap from center and dropping back—something he didn't do much of in college, operating almost exclusively from a shotgun formation. He eventually runs his backs and receivers through a 73-pattern workout showcasing a variety of drops and rollouts, and a variety of short, intermediate, and deep throws. He throws with velocity and accuracy on nearly every throw.

It should be noted that these scouts already know that RG3 can play. There's almost nothing he can do at his Pro Day to improve his stock. Griffin to the Redskins is almost a foregone conclusion. However, as much as his on-field production, they're looking at how he leads, and his interactions with teammates and coaches. Griffin seems to lead effortlessly. He also sets up his own drills, even dragging tackling dummies into place on his own.

Music throbs through the Baylor indoor facility as a variety of current and former players, media, and scouts are on hand. The crowd includes, conspicuously, Redskins head coach Mike Shanahan and owner Daniel Snyder. For what it's worth, they will attend Luck's Pro Day at Stanford the following day.

His last play is a throwback with wide receiver Kendall Wright hitting the streaking Griffin on a deep seam route. It is the icing on a nearly flawless performance. As the workout concludes, it's clear that Griffin has done what he nearly always does, which is impress everyone in his vicinity. The classic Michael Jackson track, "Thriller," plays appropriately in the background, because Griffin has thrilled. His calm is preternatural and almost unnerving.

"We had a lot of fun—that's what it's supposed to be," Griffin told reporters after the workout. "It's not supposed to be stressful. . . . That's what we try to do—lighten the mood. Have guys smiling, having fun. . . .

"My fiancée was a Broncos fan, too, so she was kind of weirded out by the whole situation, just 'cause the coach that she watched growing up was sitting right in front of her," he said of a preworkout dinner with Mike Shanahan. "But Shanahan's a great great coach, great mind, and it would be an honor to play for him."[6]

———

At Central Michigan, after bench presses and vertical jumps in the weight room, the players and scouts were herded into the indoor practice facility, and onto the bright green AstroTurf, for what has become the crown jewel of NFL talent evaluation: the 40-yard dash.

Bazuin, at 266, weighed a little lighter than his program weight of 272 and stood on his 40-yard dash time from the NFL Combine. A scout from the Baltimore Ravens secured an unused section of the field and ran him through a series of linebacker drills, thinking that Bazuin may be better suited to a stand-up role as an outside linebacker, as he may be too light to put his "hand in the dirt" as an NFL defensive lineman. The big, quiet man lumbered and puffed through the drills.

On another section of turf, the throng gathered for the all-important 40-yard dash. Even though these affairs are timed electronically, there is still a good deal of homespun superstition in NFL circles. Because of this the scouts all gathered together, nearly on top of one another, at the 40-yard line, all poised with their electronic stopwatches in hand, all convinced that their handheld times would somehow be more valid and accurate than whatever the automatic timing device generated. After each player ran his 40, the process devolved into spirited dialogue among the scouts as to what the time actually was. The irony of several middle-aged men who had flown into town, rented cars, slept in hotels, and would repeat the process over and over so that they could quibble about tenths of seconds occurred to no one.

Michael Lewis's sensational book *Moneyball* shone a light on some of the ridiculousness of baseball scouting, including its rootedness in tradition and its propensity for ignoring players who don't "look the part." Football, it seems, is still waiting for its *Moneyball* moment. Draft history would dictate that over 50 percent of the quarterbacks drafted in the first round each year are busts, meaning that either Robert Griffin or Andrew Luck could potentially be an NFL washout.

Big Joe Staley cried the first time his coach told him he would have to switch from tight end to offensive tackle. As he settled in to run his 40, millions of dollars were on the line. At 5.0 or slower, he'd be just another MAC prospect with potential. With a time of 4.9 or faster, he would be catapulted into the "first round discussion."

Staley looked gigantic, squeezed into a spandex track suit, but as he uncoiled from his stance, and his footfalls were audible on the squishy turf, we all had the feeling we were watching something special. As he crossed the line, dozens of stopwatches beeped in almost-unison. Staley's electronic time was 4.7 seconds, making him faster than most of Central's running backs and linebackers. For comparison's sake, both Tim Tebow and Cam Newton ran 4.7s at the NFL Scouting Combine.

Staley, in 4.7 seconds, had made himself a millionaire. In 4.7 seconds he vaulted past Bazuin as CMU's elite prospect, and would eventually leapfrog his teammate into the first round of the NFL draft.

I drove deep into the northern Michigan countryside a few months later to watch the 2007 NFL Draft in a pole barn with Dan Bazuin's family on the family farm. They were gracious and kind hosts, and their lack of cagey Little League Dad-ness will never be forgotten. I had an unusual feeling about the entire proceeding and until now have failed to put my finger on it. The whole thing felt, well, *sensible*. As the second-round wound down, Dan Bazuin left the party and went fishing.

Bazuin's teammate Joe Staley would become an immediate fixture at left tackle for the San Francisco 49ers, and a perennial Pro Bowler. Bazuin, a second-round draft choice of the Chicago Bears in 2007, would (due perhaps to injuries, perhaps to being overmatched) never play a down of regular season football in the NFL. He is remembered as a "bust," while the rest of the Central Michigan Chippewas present at that Pro Day have been forgotten altogether.

The quarterback class of 2007 offers an especially cautionary tale. In seven rounds, there were eleven quarterbacks selected, and all of them, for the most part, have been NFL failures, proving that even though a class may be relatively weak, teams—no doubt feeling pressure from ownership or their fan base—will still pick quarterbacks.

The first pick of that draft, JaMarcus Russell (Raiders), may go down as the biggest quarterback bust in NFL history. For what it's worth, in 2007 Russell was sensational at his Pro Day. He ran a 4.8-second 40-yard dash at 256 pounds, and impressed the man who would become his first NFL employer, then-Raiders head coach Lane Kiffin. "Obviously, I'm very impressed," Kiffin said. "We were very impressed. He had a great day. He seems very first class, very easy to get along with. No doubt he was a great leader here. That's why everybody wants him now."[7]

Russell, it was said, had prototype size, a cannon for an arm, and played in a "pro-style" offense at LSU. Still, I had some doubts. He only started two full seasons at LSU, and only attempted 797 passes, and there were whispers about his work ethic and commitment to the game.

Since 2007, Russell has started 25 NFL games and thrown only 18 touchdowns. He's currently out of football and proved to be anything but the "great leader" Kiffin saw at LSU. The second quarterback selected in the first round, Brady Quinn, has fared only slightly better, making 20 starts, and throwing 12 touchdowns. I say better only because Quinn is still employed, as a backup in Kansas City, after stops in Cleveland and Denver.

While it would be a stretch to call any of 2007's quarterbacks "successful," perhaps the most potential rests with Kevin Kolb, who has started 21 games and thrown 28 touchdown passes. While he didn't prove to be the answer in Philadelphia, he'll get another shot as a starter in Arizona. Kolb, for what it's worth, played collegiately for Griffin's college coach Art Briles, then at the University of Houston. One of the knocks on Kolb was that he played in a "gimmicky" college offense. One of the advantages to that gimmicky offense (Briles was a shotgun-spread innovator) is that it allowed him to throw a *ton* of passes as a college player. This is true of Griffin as well.

On paper, Kolb is an example of a player who has everything scouts look for. He's 6 feet 3 inches tall. He was a four-year starter for Briles at Houston, and he attempted an astonishing 1,565 passes, completing at a 61.6 percent clip, for almost 13,000 yards. So has he simply been the victim of bad circumstances thus far in the NFL? Of a Philadelphia team that never had quality receivers and was on its way down by the time he arrived? Maybe. Were Russell and Quinn the victims of being drafted into bad organizations (Oakland and Cleveland) devoid of playmaking talent and mired in a culture of losing? Probably.

Griffin, for his part, completed passes at a 67 percent clip in Briles's college offense, and brought the added dimension of a run threat. So will he end up more like JaMarcus Russell or Kevin Kolb or, preferably, neither? Is he a "safe" investment . . . or is there such a thing as a safe investment at the quarterback position where failure seems to be a 50/50 proposition? Only time and the ever-fluctuating list of surrounding circumstances will tell.

4

THE HOTTER THE HEAT, THE HARDER THE STEEL: SELLING ROBERT GRIFFIN III

W ind can be heard whistling in the background as Robert Griffin III stands outside what appears to be the Baylor football building, wearing a padded spandex shirt. The shirt, made by a company called EvoShield, is just one of the many products endorsed by Griffin before he took his first NFL snap. His trademark braids shifting a bit with the breeze, Griffin looks wide-eyed into the camera and says, "I just wanted to let you know that EvoShield has been my secret weapon for the past three years . . . and I'm excited . . . hopefully guys, you guys, will come join me as a part of the Evo Army." As he says this he pulls on an EvoShield T-shirt and salutes the camera cheesily.[1]

The video is Exhibit A of the shifting world of advertising, where online presence—via YouTube and social media—is every bit as important as the multimillion-dollar ad produced by Nike or Adidas. No longer is one television spot—Michael Jordan with Mars Blackmon, for example—the athlete's only conduit to the public and to branding. Griffin, in this poorly produced YouTube spot, is earning a paycheck and giving the public a taste of his brand and his personality.

This feels like a seismic shift from the advertising ethic of my generation (the '80s), which aimed to make the athletes seem larger than life. It was the decade of the Jumpman logo. It was the decade of Jordan soaring through the air in slow motion, which made white kids in cornfields (like me) believe they needed a pair of Nike Air Jordans more than anything else on the planet. It was the Gatorade ad. Be like Mike, meaning that Mike was so rich and famous and inaccessible that he probably floated from room to room on a cloud made of money and women and testosterone and ego. Nike wasn't just selling shoes; they were selling a dream.

Which makes the EvoShield ads even more curious. There's nothing ordinary about Robert Griffin III—athletically, at least—but in a way *everything* about him looks ordinary in this ad. There is no makeup-trailer sweat applied to his muscles, and there are no unique camera angles utilized to make him look large and magnificent. There is no throbbing rap soundtrack. He looks like what he is, which is a college student standing outside a building talking about a spandex shirt that, truth be told, probably wasn't at all his secret weapon at Baylor. Ordinary.

In Michael Jordan's ads he was rarely shown doing anything pedestrian like eating a sandwich (Griffin shills for Subway as well); and when he was shown drinking Gatorade, it was done in the context of Jordan doing something heroic, like playing with the flu against the Utah Jazz in the NBA finals, with the ad inviting the audience to worship him for it. Griffin's ads usher in a new generation—and new philosophy—of advertisements.

What makes Griffin such an effective pitchman is his relative normalcy. His gap-toothed smile. His impressive but not comic-book-ready body. The fact that he looks happy to be there. The fact that before the NFL draft in Manhattan, he agreed to make sandwiches as a promotional stunt for a Subway franchise, tossing the sandwiches over the counter to customers. Granted, he was probably being paid a small fortune to ask, "Would you like it toasted?" but still. There's an openness to Robert Griffin III and an accessibility that belies his prodigious athletic prowess. He shares this in common with Jordan.

"If you're Robert Griffin, you have to be judicious about the endorsements you do, and you have to understand what differentiates you from the rest of the marketplace," explains sports agent Eugene Lee, president of ETL & Associates, a firm featured in ESPN's 30 for 30 documentary *The Dotted Line*. "You have to have a solid understanding of your selling points, and everything—every company you work with—has to have brand integrity. It can take a lot of time and energy to make sure that the companies he endorses are consistent with the brand, and the brand is RG3."[2]

Which begs the question: What is the brand? And what was it that made Griffin the most heavily endorsed NFL draft choice in history?

"The 'It' factor has to include excellence plus championships," says Lee. "You saw it with Jordan, and you saw it with Tiger Woods. It was excellence defined by performance, and productivity at a position, and ultimately that's what companies and consumers are both looking for."[3]

————

To say that ESPN *Monday Night Football* analyst and former NFL head coach Jon Gruden has a "big personality" would be a massive understatement. In addition to the MNF brand, Gruden has created one of the biggest offseason television products in his ESPN specials titled *Gruden's QB Camp.*[4] In a rented strip-mall space in Tampa, Gruden has set up the Fired Football Coach's Association offices to serve as a makeshift studio for the programs, in which a handful of top NFL draft quarterbacking prospects are flown into town and then seated across a table from Gruden. He throws in their college film and grills them on formations, play calls, decisions, their personalities, their fashion, and anything else he can think of.

Gruden is pure football and pure television combined. He captures what is essentially great about football, and what many fans and television people miss: the fact that it's really, really fun. You can tell that Gruden is having a blast with these kids. He enjoys teaching the game; he enjoys making fun of their shirts. It's all great fun, but fans and even NFL scouts have begun to evaluate these episodes because they're so closely related to the kind of grilling that only used to go on behind closed doors at the NFL Scouting Combine.

Gruden's hair resembles that of the logo on the side of the Dutch Boy paint can, but the rest of him is über-intimidating, including eyes staring holes through Robert Griffin III. "RG3 . . . a man of style, and a man with speed," says Gruden to open the program.

"Am I right to say you'll be the fastest quarterback to ever play the position?" Gruden asks. Griffin then shifts a little and explains that he's uncomfortable talking about himself like that. But Gruden persists.

"Is anyone gonna catch me in the open field? You know, probably not," says Griffin. He's wearing an Adidas shirt that reads, "Determined." The video screen flickers with images of Griffin flying down a track ahead of his competition. "But I can throw with the best of them," he says. "I believe in my arm, and I believe I can be a quarterback, even if I didn't have the speed that I do."

One of Griffin's greatest strengths is that he shows no traces of nervousness, even in this high-pressure setting. His poise is as compelling as what is happening on screen. His attire and his demeanor are a reflection of the relaxed cool that he brings to the field. He is the nineteenth quarterback in the history of the Gruden QB School Franchise, and each player's performance on the show has given a glimpse into who they are. A year ago Cam Newton wore a polo sweater over a shirt and tie, but looked lost when Gruden put him on the chalkboard or asked him to recite one of Auburn's plays. It could be said of Griffin that he looks like himself—like he's not been coached to act like anyone else. He is also the first player in the history of the program to bring a gift—a pair of Adidas RG3 socks—for Gruden. "That's awesome," the coach says. "I'm gonna wear these every day."

Gruden is screening Baylor's historic win over Oklahoma—the first time in the school's history they'd ever beaten the Sooners. On screen, Griffin is baffling Oklahoma not only with his skill but with the tempo of the offense. Oklahoma is frequently confused and exhausted as Griffin pilots the up-tempo, no-huddle attack.

"Usually if you just watch the quarterback's demeanor, you know it's complete," Gruden says. "I've seen a lot of guys celebrate after a play . . . but I've never seen some of the stuff you do, Robert." His voice has a tinge of good-natured critique and disdain. Griffin laughs and then explains the celebrations. "It's not prepared . . . it's just out of the moment, spontaneous." He does a somersault after one touchdown. After another he sprints downfield to his teammate. "How about this one? The 360-whirlybird? You promise me these are spontaneous?" Gruden asks. "I think the lie-detector test is going off, brother."

Gruden then screens Baylor's loss to Oklahoma State, and specifically a goal-line package where Griffin throws an ugly interception over the middle. "It was the worst experience I've ever had on the goal line," says Griffin honestly. He smiles and "yes sirs" Gruden all over the place. It's endearing.

Gruden asks about the Redskins. "They seem like they need some excitement."

"I said at the Combine, I hope a team falls in love with me. . . . If Washington happens to be that team, I hope they'll be willing to grind with me and stick with me through thick and thin," he replies.

Finally, Gruden prophetically screens a play that would become a staple of the Washington Redskins offense. A play-action fake off the zone-read in which Griffin lines up in a shotgun formation, fakes a handoff to his running back—which pulls the defensive end and line-backers in—and then hits his receiver on a slant-and-go. The receiver looks like he's running the slant, which draws the safety up, then breaks into a "go" (straight downfield), leaving the safety in his wake. It's a play that only works well with a running threat like RG3 in the back-field. The Redskins would make a living on it. It's the play—more than any other—that will lead them to the playoffs in Griffin's rookie year.

Later, Gruden puts Griffin on the field, as he does with all the prospects. Griffin walks to the field in a spandex shirt with one long sleeve and one short sleeve with metallic accents. He looks like a robo-quarterback and even sounds like one as the medallions around his neck clang when he moves around. On anyone else, the getup would feel excessive and ridiculous. Griffin, somehow, pulls it off.

"What do you got on your left elbow there?" Gruden asks of Griffin's sartorial choice.

"It's a little sleeve," Griffin replies. "It's a party on the left hand; it's all business on the right."

Gruden turns to the camera and smirks, incredulous.

———

Let's talk about socks, baby. Griffin has built a brand from silly, graphic socks like SpongeBob, Angry Birds, and Superman. He wore the aforementioned Superman socks to the Heisman presentation and, according to a *Forbes* report, "After he won the Heisman, the Superman socks he wore—produced by Texas-based Bioworld Merchandising Inc. for $14.99 per pair—were sold out around the Internet. Many pairs were purchased for well above $50."[5]

After mainstreaming the graphic sock, Griffin teamed with his shoe sponsor, Adidas, to produce a burgundy-and-gold (Redskins colors) sock that reads, "Go Chase Your Dream." There are also socks on eBay fetching upward of $50 or more with RG3 slogans like "No Pressure, No Diamonds" and "Unbelievably Believable." And according to a *USA Today* piece, Griffin apparently handed out the socks to trick-or-treaters on Halloween night.[6] Is this just the kind of playful exuberance that most twenty-two-year-old kids would indulge in if they had a shoe company at their disposal and, relatively speaking, all the money in the world? Maybe. Or it's not outside the realm of possibility that this is part of a savvier marketing plan that presents Griffin as both a serious athlete and at the same time a kind, playful, almost self-deprecating athlete by whom you're not intimidated and from whom you'd like to buy nearly anything.

The fact is that Griffin's sock cottage-industry is working because Griffin is working. If the Redskins were 3-10 and Griffin had struggled mightily as a rookie, the socks would be the kind of silly distraction writers would use as proof of Griffin's "lack of commitment to the game" and "lack of seriousness." But because he's working, the socks, the commercials, and all of the off-field commitments are working.

The fact is, Madison Avenue and middle America both saw glimpses of the "It" factor when Griffin ascended the stage at the Downtown Athletic Club in New York City to accept the Heisman Trophy.

He let out an audible "whoof" (excitement? fatigue?) as he took his spot behind the podium wearing a suit that was nice but not draft-day nice (which is to say, not draft-day ostentatious). He made a joke about his socks (Superman, with little capes around his calves), and the audience guffawed like good, obedient audiences do when they're in the presence of greatness. His large, wide-set eyes darted to and fro. His braids dangled in front of them occasionally, but there's something winsome and trustworthy and playful about his braids, as opposed to the ominous dreadlocks of Ricky Williams or Lennox Lewis. Or perhaps is middle America is just ready to buy a sub sandwich from a guy who looks like Bob Marley, whereas they weren't when Ricky won his Heisman?

He said nothing more spiritual than "God always has a plan and it's our job to fulfill it." He thanked his parents, who beamed from the audience, and acknowledged his sisters, his niece, and his fiancée. He made eye contact. He didn't mumble. There was nothing especially unique about what he said, but there was something unique about the way he said it—and that uniqueness can be summed up in a word: *authentic.* It seemed authentic. It seemed as unscripted as a twenty-two-year-old's trophy acceptance speech can possibly be.

Griffin said of the experience that it's "unbelievably believable." "The great coach Art Briles always says that great things only come with great effort . . . as we say, the hotter the heat, the harder the steel. No pressure, no diamonds. We compete, and we are Baylor."

During the season following RG3's departure, Baylor was back to being Baylor—which is to say around .500 and mostly forgettable. Robert Griffin III proved to be a program builder. He proved to be a player who can put a program on the map. Washington needs him to do it again.

WHAT THE REDSKINS NEEDED
WAS QUARTERBACKING

The Washington Redskins entered Week 17 of the 2011 season at a disappointing 5-11, playing in one of those mostly forgotten end-of-season matchups against another NFC East franchise that has perennially disappointed, the Philadelphia Eagles. On a rare sunny winter afternoon in Philadelphia, the Redskins started Rex Grossman, who on the season had thrown for 15 touchdowns and 19 interceptions. Grossman's pedestrian numbers proved to be the writing on the wall—namely, that the Redskins would be going in another direction at quarterback the following season, which had become a familiar refrain for Washington fans.

Grossman occasionally shared the job in 2011 with John Beck, for whom there was a momentary surge of excitement in Washington. But Beck was 0-3 in his starts, with 2 touchdowns and 4 interceptions. In one of the more decisive draft-day moves in recent memory, Beck was unceremoniously released the moment the Redskins took their second quarterback in four rounds.

Since Doug Williams led the Redskins to Super Bowl glory in 1988, and since the able but unspectacular Mark Rypien game-managed the Redskins to their own Super Bowl title a few years later in 1992, the list of Redskins quarterbacks has been long and unsatisfying.

The list includes three failed first-round draft choices. Heath Shuler—an undersized but dynamic running quarterback from Tennessee—only started 13 games for Washington and ended his career with more than twice as many interceptions (33) than touchdowns (15). In 2002, über-involved owner Daniel Snyder forced then–head coach Steve Spurrier into selecting Tulane's Patrick Ramsey, and then forced Spurrier to play him, resulting in a short but awkward stay in Washington for both player and coach. Ramsey never developed in four seasons of intermittent starts and was soon shown the door. Finally, in 2005, the Redskins selected Auburn's Jason Campbell near the end of the first round. Campbell started for two full seasons and put up some solid numbers, but the wins never followed. He posted a 4-12 record in his final season as a starter and lacked the "It" factor needed to helm a franchise and engineer victories. He has settled as a high-end backup in Chicago after another failed starting stint in Oakland.

In between there were stopgaps like Gus Frerotte, John Friesz, and Tony Banks. There were short stints by quarterbacks who had success in other places, like Rich Gannon, who won a Super Bowl in Oakland, and Trent Green, who provided quality starts for St. Louis and Kansas City. There were over-the-hill veterans with Super Bowl rings like Jeff Hostetler and over-the-hill veterans like Jeff George who had never met expectations elsewhere. And then there was the bizarre Shane Matthews and Danny Wuerffel era, in which Spurrier thought he could recreate his high-octane Florida Gators offenses on the pro level with the same personnel. He was wrong.

It could be argued that by the end of 2011, the Redskins were nearing two decades of wandering in the proverbial quarterbacking desert. They needed not only an able athlete but also a face for the franchise. Owner Daniel Snyder's freewheeling spending in free agency had turned up nothing but big-name busts like Sean Gilbert and, most recently, Albert Haynesworth, who repeatedly failed Shanahan's preseason conditioning tests and was summarily dumped.

The previous two decades stand in sharp contrast to a history filled largely with successful and charismatic quarterbacks. With his iconic single-bar face mask, Notre Dame product Joe Theismann enjoyed an almost decade-long run as the starter from the mid-'70s through the mid-'80s. The Theismann-era 'Skins were a collection of personalities—names like John Riggins, The Smurfs (the club's diminutive receivers), The Hogs (the club's massive and popular linemen), and the silver-tongued Theismann himself, who was equal parts Hollywood and old-school (see: single-bar face mask and lots of busted-out teeth). At any rate, his era really represented the last extended excitement generated by the position.

Before Theismann, the position was held down by popular veteran Billy Kilmer and also Sonny Jurgensen, who is a member of the Pro Football Hall of Fame, was a five-time Pro Bowl selection, and about whom legendary coach Vince Lombardi once said, "He is the best quarterback I've ever seen."[1]

Even Norm Snead, who preceded the quarterbacks above, repre-sented Washington in the Pro Bowl in 1962 and 1963. Week 17 of 2011 provides context for just how badly the Redskins needed a leader, but also the nucleus of quality players that would key the transition and play a role in the ascension of RG3.

Across the field on that December afternoon in 2011 stood Mike Vick, who is perhaps one of Robert Griffin's stylistic ancestors and who was (unbeknownst to him at the time) nearing the end of his confusing run as Philadelphia's starter. He returned from a suspension and jail time on a dogfighting conviction in Week 3 of 2009, acting as a decoy wide receiver and a backup to incumbent starting QB Kevin Kolb; but it was Vick's stellar 2010 season that earned him favor with Philly fans and cemented him as the starter. In 2010, Vick threw for 3,018 yards with 21 touchdowns and only 6 interceptions—a level of ball security that was previously unheard of for Vick. There was talk of him really developing as a passer, and he didn't throw an interception until Week 7 of the season.

Vick and head coach Andy Reid seemed to be inextricably linked, as both carried the burdens of fame and pressure. Reid had five NFC Championship appearances on his résumé, but only one Super Bowl appearance and a loss to New England. Another disappointing season in Philly meant that Reid's goodwill—seemingly endless a few years previous—now had a shelf life. The Eagles needed to win—and win soon—and would need to wait another year to see if they could do so with Vick at quarterback.

Vick, though always heavily hyped, had numbers that were eerily similar to Grossman's in 2011, completing under 60 percent of his throws and throwing for only 15 scores (with 13 picks) on the season. Even Vick's definitive dark visor, while once looking so flashy, just seemed a little outdated.

The game started sluggishly, with both teams going three-and-out on their first two drives, and Vick going 1-5 in the first quarter. Meanwhile, in Carolina, rookie quarterback Cam Newton—about whom there were major red flags coming out of Auburn—was putting the finishing touches on a Herculean rookie season that would perhaps influence Washington's direction in the upcoming draft. The first overall pick in the 2011 draft, Newton threw for over 4,000 yards as a rookie, adding 21 touchdowns through the air to go with an astonishing 706 yards and 14 touchdowns on the ground. More importantly, Newton was doing what football pundits had said couldn't be done—running a version of a college offense (spread option) at the pro level.

The Redskins, meanwhile, lacked playmakers on both sides of the football. Their bright spots included undersized veteran linebacker London Fletcher, who had 163 tackles coming into the game and was Washington's only representative in the Pro Bowl. The defense featured promising rookie Ryan Kerrigan—an outside linebacker out of Purdue—and superstar outside linebacker Brian Orakpo, who failed to make the Pro Bowl. The offense, by contrast, was stunningly devoid of playmakers. Washington's best wide receiver was the diminutive and aging Santana Moss, while the running game featured a Roy Helu/Tim Hightower/Evan Royster backfield-by-committee that wasn't exactly striking fear into offensive coordinators. Overall, Shanahan's backs had trouble staying healthy and hadn't seemed to settle into his legendary zone-run schemes; but Royster provided the bright spot of the first half for Washington, ripping off an impressive 28-yard run in which he made several defenders miss.

Sadly, though, Washington's defining moment of the half came with a minute remaining—when unheralded Philadelphia receiver Chad Hall caught a Vick pass in the flat, then broke halfhearted tackles by linebacker Perry Riley and high-priced cornerback DeAngelo Hall on his way to the end zone. To end the half, Grossman would hit Jabar Gaffney deep over the middle, but the field goal team would fail to get onto the field with enough time to kick. Grossman finished the half 12-24, but only 1-7 on third down. The Redskins were failing to make plays when plays needed to be made.

The second half brought more disappointment as the offense sputtered. The defense gave up a backside screen to Eagles tight end Brent Celek for a score and a 9-yard run by backup running back Dion Lewis to put the game out of reach at 34-10. The building blocks were few and far between for Washington. Could Evan Royster develop into a full-time back? Was tight end Fred Davis explosive enough to give Washington high-end production like Gronkowski and Gonzalez of the Patriots? Did the team have a true number one at wide receiver, with the journeyman Gaffney and the undersized Moss? How good was Brian Orakpo, really?

In 2011, Mike Shanahan's Super Bowl success in Denver seemed a long way off, and he would have to answer these pressing questions, and others, in order to keep his job. Before 2012, Shanahan would enact a housecleaning, parting ways with veterans like Gaffney, Chris Cooley, Mike Sellers, Donte Stallworth, and Tim Hightower. He seemed committed to recreating the team in his own image, with his own players; and that rebirth would need to start at the quarterback position.

————

Dressed in black spandex shorts and an orange Under Armour tank top emblazoned with his NFL Scouting Combine player number, Robert Griffin settled into his sprinter's stance at the starting line of the 40-yard dash. "You can tell he's a track guy," said former New York Giants defensive back and NFL Network track analyst Mike Mayock on the network telecast.

The NFL Scouting Combine happens each year in the month of February as collegiate prospects arrive in Indianapolis—by invitation only—to be evaluated by every team in the NFL. It has become a media hallmark of the NFL's brilliant offseason calendar—a calendar that is calibrated to keep fan interest peaking throughout the year. At the combine, each prospect is evaluated in the 40-yard dash, vertical jump, standing broad jump, pro shuttle, three-cone agility drill, bench press (optional for quarterbacks), an intelligence test, and a full array of passing drills.

Griffin's 6-foot-2-inch (a little short?) and 223-pound body revealed little to no body fat and no wasted motion as he exploded out of his stance. Lucas Oil Stadium, per usual for the NFL Combine, felt empty and quiet. The stands were sprinkled with scouts in officially licensed team gear, and the field was sprinkled with other nervous-looking players wearing Under Armour sweat suits and waiting for the four seconds that would justify their existence and validate their hard work. Players literally run, jump, and throw for dollars, as their performance here has a direct correlation to their draft status in April. The league knows that this is the best kind of reality television, and although the event itself is closed to anyone except league personnel, media coverage of it in recent years has become manic.

His footfalls were audible on the FieldTurf, and as Griffin exploded through the finish line, Mayock simply said, "Wow." Unofficially he was timed at 4.38 seconds—territory that had previously been reserved for speedsters like Deion Sanders, DeAngelo Hall, and Darrell Green. Incidentally, all are cornerbacks and current or former Redskins. Officially, Griffin clocked in at 4.41, but his speed and athleticism were only a portion of a dazzling combine and Pro Day performance.

According to Terry Shea's quarterbacking bible, *Eyes Up*, quarterbacks are tested on the following:

1. Grip. The quarterback grips a football for a ground-level camera shot intended to show the size of a quarterback's hands.

2. Drops and throwing mechanics. Quarterbacks perform back-out and three-, five-, and seven-step crossover drops, delivering balls to stationary receivers.

3. Rollout. Quarterbacks roll to their right and left, pulling up at the numbers and delivering a ball 20 yards downfield to a stationary receiver.

4. Hook up with receivers. Finally, quarterbacks throw quick slants, outs, digs (a deeper "in" route), curls, gos, post-corners, and deep outs to live receivers.[2]

In addition to the on-field activity, players are available for fifteen-minute interviews with teams. According to Shea, many teams reach an early judgment on players based on their fifteen-minute interviews. In 1998, the last season in which there was a tightly contested duel for the first-round spot between quarterbacks Ryan Leaf and Peyton Manning, Leaf apparently missed his appointment with the Indianapolis Colts, who ended up selecting Manning. Manning, by contrast, arrived at his appointment with a legal pad and "interviewed" the Colts—asking extensive and detailed questions about offensive philosophy and person-nel.[3] The Colts knew they had their man.

"How you present yourself [posture, eye contact, self-confidence] is as important as the responses to the questions themselves," Shea writes. "Demonstrate confidence, but a touch of humility goes a long way."[4]

Writes Shea, questions can range from football "Xs and Os" to leadership scenarios. He helps prepare quarterback prospects by having them answer questions like, "For your first play as an NFL rookie, what play do you want sent in?" and "How will you handle an out-of-control veteran in your offensive huddle?" Players are sometimes even asked to list every play they can remember from their college offense. When he was with the Kansas City Chiefs, Shea was asked to evaluate quarter-backs according to a seven-part rubric:

1. Is he coachable and is he available?
2. Confidence: Does he believe in himself?
3. Competitor/Loves the Challenge: Is he at his best when he needs to be?
4. Poise: How does he react in stressful situations?
5. Skill: Is he able to execute his job, not just be a part of it?
6. Condition: Is he physically, mentally, and emotionally tough? His performance should never vary regardless of the situation.
7. Passion and Energy: Does he enjoy practicing and playing the game of football?[5]

As the pre-draft process unfolded, it was clear that Griffin was off the charts in each category, wowing media and scouts with his interpersonal skills as well as his athleticism. His draft-season adversary was equally sensa-tional Stanford quarterback Andrew Luck, son of a former NFL quarterback (Oliver Luck) and a more traditionally prototypical NFL quarterback. At 6 feet 4 inches and 234 pounds, Luck stood tall in the pocket and ran a tra-ditional pro-style offense at Stanford, where he threw for over 9,000 yards with 82 touchdown passes and only 22 interceptions. The words *smart*, *poised*, and *polished* continued to surface in connection with Luck, but some questioned his upside. To be fair, these were the same questions posited about Peyton Manning in 1998, and his upside seems to have worked out fine for all involved. To his poise and polish, Luck added a sneaky athleti-cism. He ran 4.7 in the 40 at the combine (same as Cam Newton and Tim Tebow) and ran for 957 yards and 7 touchdowns at Stanford—not exactly the numbers of an unathletic statue in the pocket.

———

The occasion of Robert Griffin's selection by the Washington Redskins was probably the worst-kept secret in sports. The Redskins pulled off one of the biggest trades in draft history to move up to the number two spot, swapping first-round positions with the Rams and giving them first-round picks in 2013 and 2014 and a second-round pick in the 2012 draft. As for Griffin, he said all the right things pre-draft. "I'm going to assimilate to the culture of the team that picks me, on the field and in the locker room," he told *Sports Illustrated*. "I'm not coming into the NFL with, let's say, five plays from Baylor that I love and saying to the offensive coordinator, 'Hey, we have to run these.' That's not my job. I just want to fit in."[6]

Redskins coach Mike Shanahan said that drafting RG3 was "nearly a sure thing" before the draft.[7] This was reinforced by the fact that Griffin spurned the Colts' request for a pre-draft workout, feeling certain that they were going to draft Andrew Luck and perhaps communicating his own desire to play in the nation's capital.

Washington Post sportswriter Mark Maske reported on the selection: "'We tried to keep it secret as long as we could,' Redskins Coach Mike Shanahan said at Redskins Park soon after the pick was made, describing team officials as 'elated' with the selection. 'He wants to be the guy,' Shanahan added. 'He's going to do everything he possibly can to be successful. You don't have to be around him very long to figure that out.'"[8]

Griffin's father gave an interview in the lead-up to the NFL draft and spoke of the importance of family. "I grew up with mom and dad. I had an expectation. . . . Robert and my daughter—the same thing. We have that one, inner-group connection . . . the fact that we all, you know, believe in family. And that's been very important to us.

"I tell Robert that, number one, you know, remember faith first. . . . When everybody else fails, God is still there for you," he said. When asked about the moment he felt Robert may have had limitless athletic potential, he talked about Robert's youth basketball league, where he played against kids who were years older and inches taller. "Robert was nine. . . . Coach put Robert in the game and Robert went to work. He made a move like Dr. J."[9]

He went on to talk about how in tenth grade his son said he wanted to be a lawyer, and how they almost sent Robert to the University of Houston because of the opportunities it would have provided for his law career. All of that seems quaint in light of the grandeur and spectacle of the NFL draft, which has become must-see television for NFL fans. First-round coverage of the 2012 draft would draw over 25 million viewers on ESPN and the NFL Network combined.

Former NFL coach Brian Billick, in his book *More Than a Game*, described his experience with the draft this way: "As I entered the grand ballroom of New York's Radio City Music Hall for the 2008 NFL draft I felt as if I were walking into Herod's Temple. The place reeked of money."[10]

Griffin was photographed and videotaped for ESPN's intro/outro sets in which the players are shown lifting weights, throwing a ball, and mugging for the camera. It's all intended to give the event a larger-than-life feel. It works. Also larger-than-life were Griffin's endorsement deals before the draft, as he inked agreements with Adidas, Castrol, Subway, and EA Sports before he was even affiliated with an NFL club.

Griffin wore burgundy-and-gold striped Adidas socks and a light blue suit to the draft at Radio City Music Hall in New York. As NFL commissioner Roger Goodell strode to the podium, there was very little suspense. "With the second overall pick in the NFL draft, the Washington Redskins select Robert Griffin III."

A few miles away, in Washington DC, draft parties exploded with excitement and hope. Grown men wearing Redskins jerseys were beside themselves with platitudes. "RG3, we love you already! Bring one home for us!" "My favorite thing about RG3 is his socks!" exclaimed another fan. "There's nothing he can't do!" said another.[11] It was a moment full of hope, but also full of pressure and expectation, because a fan's love is the very definition of *conditional* love. At another draft party, Redskins fans joyfully smashed a Jerry Jones (Cowboys owner) piñata. Griffin highlight footage spun on repeat on ESPN and the NFL Network. We saw countless versions of his late touchdown pass heroics against Oklahoma—the play where he scrambled left, got smacked in the face, and still threw up a touchdown pass.

"How can anyone not let that go to their head?" asked my wife, watching it unfold. "From now on, everyone he meets will love him for this, and not for who he really is." Leave it to a woman, my wife, to boil this whole thing down to its essence. I wanted to tell her that it's all just a part of the hype, that most men would kill to be loved "for this." But she's right. The money, the fame, the shallow "love" of a fan all presented a potential assault on young Griffin's character.

"I'm not going to any award shows or doing any commercials during the season," Griffin said during an introductory press conference. "All that's done. I did my work in the offseason, whether it was with marketing or just football work, making sure I stayed in shape and stayed on top of the playbook. I made sure I did all of that, while at the same time making sure I handled my business."[12]

"I'm real excited," he said in a conference call with reporters. "A team finally fell in love with me. They want me for who I am, and I can't wait to go play for them."[13]

ROBERT GRIFFIN III IS SENSATIONAL (BUT SO IS KYLE SHANAHAN)

There is no opening day in sports as exciting and meaningful as opening day in the NFL. The uniforms are new, gleaming, and sensational—this year made more sensational by the fact that sports-fashion trendsetter Nike has taken over NFL uniform design under its Pro Combat imprint, and the spandex-inspired fabrics make the athletes look even more encased in their uniforms and impressive than usual.

For RG3, training camp and the preseason were remarkable, setting expectations at a fever pitch for his opener. According to tight end Chris Cooley (who would be released and later re-signed by the club), Griffin's most impressive preseason work came off the field. Cooley said, "Griffin walked into the Redskins' locker room and immediately established credibility and leadership. Young players idolize him. Veterans respect him." The ESPN.com article referred to Griffin as "more mature than his age."[1]

"He's so real," Cooley told CBS Sports. "This is who he is. I sit next to him in the team meetings, and there isn't a guy on the team he doesn't have a relationship with. Not one. He talks to everyone, he shares part of himself with everyone. He sends texts to everyone. Griff is our leader. People wonder if he's the same guy they see being interviewed or in the commercials. He is. He is the kind of person you want to follow. It's all real.

"He's an extremely intelligent person," Cooley continued. "He graduated high school in three years. He graduated college as an undergrad and had almost completed his master's. His mind works fast."[2] The veteran tight end would ultimately be a camp casualty—cut before the season began, replaced by younger tight ends including Niles Paul, Logan Paulsen, and emerging star Fred Davis.

Intent on establishing his leadership, Griffin invited teammates to his home in Waco, Texas, before training camp to work on skills and establish relationships. He made believers out of teammates on the field as well. "You hear about his speed, but until you go against it, you don't actually know what you're against," veteran linebacker London Fletcher told CBS. "He has a rocket of an arm. He has the right mentality as far as preparation. . . . When you face him, the speed is what will definitely shock you, and then his talent as well."[3]

His preseason debut at Buffalo was pretty quiet, with Griffin muffing a handoff and failing to get a first down on his first series. But his third series revealed 3 straight completions, culminating in a 20-yard scoring strike to Pierre Garçon, who quickly became a favored target in training camp. Griffin's pass would be the only scoring play of the game for the Redskins, who prevailed by a 7-6 margin.

Preseason also brought a much-anticipated showdown with number one overall pick and Colts quarterback Andrew Luck, who was making believers of his own in Indianapolis. Both quarterbacks acquitted themselves well, with Luck throwing a pretty 61-yard touchdown pass to

T. Y. Hilton, and Griffin leading a couple of scoring drives. Both players validated their respective franchises' excitement in Washington's 30-17 win.

———

Robert Griffin III makes his first pro start on the road at New Orleans against a team that has lost its head coach (Sean Payton) to an ugly bounty scandal that dominated NFL headlines for the majority of the offseason. In a nutshell, the Saints were accused of putting bounties on the heads of opposing players—mostly quarterbacks—and rewarding defensive players for injuring their opponents. It's an uneasy truce that we as fans make with NFL football. We know it's excessively violent, we even celebrate the violence, but a situation like this creates an awkward tension between the violence that's there and the image that the league wants to create and promote. Payton, as the on-field leader of the Saints, was offered as a sacrifice, along with the perpetrating coach (defensive coordinator Gregg Williams) and a handful of Saints players, making the hamstrung Saints a tantalizing Week 1 opponent for a rookie QB with talent and some weaponry at his disposal.

On the sidelines for New Orleans is an interim head coach named Aaron Kromer who will be coaching his first game as a head coach at any level. Across the field is Mike Shanahan, who is beginning his third season and has compiled an 11-21 record for an unremarkable .343 winning percentage and to whom the phrase "make or break" could apply. The Redskins will need to see vast improvement, if not a playoff appearance, in order to salvage the Shanahan regime. As always, on the sideline, he looks unhappy and mildly uncomfortable. Joyous exuberance, while demonstrated by some coaches, is not a hallmark of the Shanahan approach. Shanahan has the appearance and demeanor of a professor, and has the genius reputation to accompany it, although the clock is ticking for that genius to reestablish itself.

Warming up across the field is the man charged with keeping the Saints' ship afloat in the interim, quarterback Drew Brees, whose class and consistency has made him a "face of the franchise" quarterback that all teams crave. Always consistent on the field and never an embarrassment off it, Brees was absolutely sensational a season ago, throwing for 5,476 yards and 46 touchdowns. He also hit a ridiculous 71.2 percent of his passes and is the kind of quarterback who makes stars out of his receivers and tight ends—elevating the numbers of players like Pierre Thomas and making stars out of players like tight end Jimmy Graham, who was better known as a basketball player at the University of Miami.

When Griffin jogs onto the field with the offense, he is the first rookie quarterback to start on opening day for Washington since Norm Snead in 1961, which is remarkable given the parade of first-round draft picks the 'Skins have spent on signal callers (including Heath Shuler, Patrick Ramsey, and Jason Campbell). Joining him in the backfield is fellow rookie Alfred Morris: a sixth-round choice from Florida Atlantic whom Shanahan hopes can master his zone-run schemes and follow in the footsteps of other unheralded 1,000-yard Shanahan backs like Mike Anderson and Olandis Gary.

Griffin's first pro pass is a short completion to Pierre Garçon, who represented the team's biggest offseason acquisition and upgraded a woeful receiving corps. Garçon, groomed at tiny Division III powerhouse Mount Union, played in a Super Bowl in Indianapolis and had effectively taken over the "deep threat" mantle from veteran Reggie Wayne. Still, Garçon's comfort level and rapport with Griffin will determine his worth in Washington, and his acquisition is proof that Shanahan is beginning to overhaul the roster in his own image.

"Pierre is a guy that enjoys blocking as much as receiving, so he's a very physical wide receiver," he said in a weekly press conference. "He's not afraid to hit a safety, hit a corner. Not a lot of wide receivers have that type of mind-set." He continued, "People talk about wide receivers in general. In Denver, you talk about Rod Smith and Ed McCaffrey who took as much pride in the running game as they did in the passing game. Jerry Rice and John Taylor did the same thing. Usually the great ones take the most pride in the things they do."[4]

On the same drive, Griffin flashes his running ability on a college-style read-option that goes for 12 yards. The play is both a tantalizing look at his potential, but also an uncomfortable reminder of his fragility. From the waist down, he is built like an Olympic sprinter/defensive end, but his upper body, which of course includes the throwing arm, is slight and will take a pounding if Shanahan continues to deploy him as a runner.

On his third play as a pro, Griffin already shows above-average play-action sleight of hand, freezing the defense on a run fake and hitting Garçon. The play-action ability was something he showed at Baylor and was a major selling point with NFL personnel men. He hits Garçon again for 9, and what develops is an expertly crafted opening drive for a rookie quarterback. Like some teams, the Redskins "script," or predetermine, the first several offensive play calls of each game. This is done to give players—especially young players—a comfort level with the game plan and a foreknowledge of what's going to be called when the "bullets are real." The scripting philosophy began with legendary coach Bill Walsh when he was an assistant with the Cincinnati Bengals. He later perfected the philosophy as a head coach in San Francisco, where he aimed to give young quarterback Joe Montana confidence going into games.

"We have the first 20 plays scripted," explained Mike Shanahan in a midweek press conference. "Sometimes it's 15. Sometimes it's 20. Sometimes it's a little bit more. The players have a good idea of what's going to be called in the first quarter, first quarter and a half, so they can go through all of the adjustments that they need to make against different defenses and possible audibles."[5]

Each of his scripted throws are short—lots of slants and bubble screens—scripted to build his confidence while not exposing a suspect offensive line with deep drops and long-developing plays. The drive has the added benefit of taking time off the clock and whittling away at Brees's own opportunities with the football.

When he converts a key third and 5 to slot receiver and return specialist Brandon Banks, Griffin is a perfect 5 for 5, and the drive ends in a field goal by Billy Cundiff.

On his second drive, Griffin settles in for his first play under center, as the entire first drive unfolds from a shotgun, which Griffin used almost exclusively in college. With three receivers lined up in a bunch formation, Griffin drops back, facing a fierce New Orleans pass rush in his face. He sets his feet and throws a laser over the middle to Garçon, who dashes untouched into the end zone as Griffin pulls himself off the turf and runs downfield for a chest-bump with his new receiver. The pass serves notice that Griffin is more than a runner, and that he can see opportunities downfield and deliver an accurate football.

"I know how pumped I was and how pumped our team was," said Kyle Shanahan of the scoring play. "It took us until Week 16 to run a touchdown in last year on a reception and it happened in the first quarter of this game. It wasn't a small one, it was a big one. When you get plays like that, I think it changes the whole aspect of the game—coverages get softer, people get more scared, people get confident. It makes it a lot easier on everybody."[6]

Griffin ends the quarter a perfect 7 for 7 with 123 yards and a touch-down. The game plan appears balanced, with 7 runs and 7 passes thus far with the quarterback showing preternatural poise on the road in a loud, hostile environment.

A second-quarter play-action rollout shows still more evidence of Griffin's unique skill set. He extends the play with his feet, eluding defenders and throwing a 26-yard strike across his body and across the field with accuracy. His first incompletion doesn't occur until 12:24 of the second quarter.

On a third and goal from the 5-yard line, in a shotgun with three receivers to the right of the formation, Griffin coolly hits Aldrick Robinson on a slant for the score. He slow-points to the sky. It seems rehearsed in the mode of Cam Newton's "Superman" or Tim Tebow's "Tebowing."

———

With a 20-14 lead to open the third quarter, Griffin hits veteran wide-out Santana Moss for 14 yards. He then accurately connects with Josh Morgan for 21 (again off play-action), then mixes in a zone run to Morris, who always seems to fall forward and already has the look of a Shanahan back. On a courageous call on fourth down and inches, Griffin throws deep and draws a pass-interference call to extend the drive. They score a play later on a Morris plunge from a yard out, and the extra point makes the score 27-14. For the first time there is the reality that a rookie quarter-back could light up Drew Brees and the Saints in their own house.

Griffin, who by the end of the third quarter has amassed 258 passing yards and 2 touchdowns, stands in stark statistical contrast to his rookie counterparts, all of whom are struggling in their openers. Luck has gone

14-34 with 2 picks; Dolphins rookie Ryan Tannehill has thrown 3 interceptions; and Browns first-rounder Brandon Weeden has 3 picks to go with only 93 passing yards.

Meanwhile, Brees is doing what Brees does, which is passing the football and keeping New Orleans competitive in the fourth quarter. He hits receiver Lance Moore deep on a fourth-down play, and a Darren Sproles 2-point conversion shrinks the gap to 33-25 Redskins with 6:19 to go. The next time Brees has the football, he's picked by Redskins safety DeJon Gomes, who returns the ball 49 yards to the Saints 3 on a high, ill-advised pass. Alfred Morris runs off left tackle for the score—bulling his way in and freight-training David Hawthorne in the process, making the score 40-25 with the extra point. For the sake of perspective, it is the first time since 2005 the Redskins have scored 40 points in a game.

The final score is 40-32, and the final numbers tell the story of a brilliantly conceived game plan by offensive coordinator Kyle Shanahan. The time-of-possession battle was ruled by Washington (39:10 to 20:50), and Morris contributed 96 yards and 2 TDs on the ground. Mike Shanahan would say the following week, "He is a young back with a lot of ability. He can hit the hole extremely hard and has the lateral quickness to make you miss, but he's got the power to run over people. That's a pretty good combination. He's got a good feel for the game. I don't think blocking is too big for him either. It seems like he enjoys blocking, as well as running the football. After the game you can tell that it was just a game. A lot of guys get intimidated in their first football game in the National Football League, especially on the road in that environment. You could see that it wasn't too big for him."[7]

Griffin's debut, meanwhile, was nearly historic, as only Cam Newton passed for more yardage (422) in a rookie debut. Griffin finished with 320 yards passing, another 42 on the ground, and 2 touchdowns. The play calling was equal parts protective of Griffin and ultra-aggressive and confident when it needed to be.

"I was real pleased with how he played the whole game," said Kyle Shanahan afterward. "You guys know the big passes he made—the big one to [wide receiver] Pierre [Garçon] just hanging in there when they were bringing in one more than we could pick up. He hung in there, took the hit, got it off, and there was a 90-yard touchdown because of it. There are also a few times in the game where he called some shot plays that weren't there and it was nice for him not to just throw it just because we called it. He was able to go to the next guy and be smart with the ball—not always just taking the big play, just let the game come to him."[8]

"Letting the game come to him" is one of the most oft-used press-conference clichés in sports. In reality, Griffin did anything but. He seized his starting opportunity as definitively as Newton did the year before, and as definitively as any other rookie quarterback in history. A message had been sent. The Redskins had their quarterback, and they knew how to use him.

7

WARRIORS AND HUMANS: ON INJURY, MARCUS LATTIMORE, AND RG3

Each time I stand on the sideline for an NFL game, I'm reminded of how brutal and violent a sport I'm witnessing. I've sat ringside for heavyweight boxing matches and have even (regrettably and weirdly) had to sit "cage-side" for MMA bouts. But in my opinion, they're all tame compared to the speed, collisions, and carnage on display at an NFL game.

By Week 2, when the Redskins traveled again to face the Rams, RG3 was a full-blown sensation. The network telecast opened with a graphic reading "RGIII Mania!" accompanied by a picture of Griffin on his butt with both index fingers in the air after throwing a touchdown pass. It's a move known as "Griffining," which is a play on "Tebowing™" and which, if we're lucky, will never catch on.

Against the Rams, Griffin faces another former Heisman winner and former Terry Shea disciple, Sam Bradford—who has toiled in semi-obscurity for a franchise trying to find itself. The Rams have something to be excited about, however: landing former Titans coach Jeff Fisher.

But on the first play from scrimmage, Rams receiver Danny Amendola is stripped by Redskins linebacker Perry Riley. The ball is returned by Josh Wilson for a touchdown. However, after two plays from scrimmage, the Redskins are up a touchdown and down a defensive lineman—losing Adam Carriker to an injury that would keep him out for the season. The game will also claim star linebacker Brian Orakpo to a shoulder injury, and the Redskins will mourn their loss of a pass rush for the rest of the season. A team that can't afford to lose stars is now down three: Carriker, Orakpo, and Griffin's security blanket, Pierre Garçon, who leaves the opener with a torn ligament in his foot.

A red-zone series illustrates the fact that when Griffin becomes a runner, he's going to get rocked like a runner. He is blasted out of bounds after racing to the corner and, upon standing, drops an expletive and shouts, cognizant of the league's new helmet-to-helmet rules, "He's leading with his helmet!" He notches his first career rush TD a few plays later, keeping the ball on a ride option play with running back Alfred Morris.

On the next series, after two short passes to Santana Moss and Josh Morgan, he hits Leonard Hankerson deep over the middle on a simple stutter-go route, with Hankerson torching his former Miami teammate Janoris Jenkins for the score. At this point, the Fox analysts are beside themselves, saying of Griffin, "He has style without even trying!" and "There's an aura about him."

Bradford and Danny Amendola battle valiantly to keep the Rams in the game, picking apart the Redskins' soft-zone defense. The same defense that brought tons of pressure on Drew Brees in Week 1 is generating no rush on Bradford—no doubt missing Orakpo and Carriker. Orakpo, 6 feet 4 inches and 257 pounds, and possessing 4.63 speed in the 40-yard dash, represents the kind of dynamic pass rusher that NFL teams covet. A two-time Pro Bowler with 29.5 sacks on his career, he's a player who disrupts the opponent's passing game by overwhelming the left tackle across him and changing protection schemes. Teams have been searching for these dynamic outside backers since Lawrence Taylor of the Giants permanently changed the position in the 1980s.

On a second and goal from the 7 in the third quarter, Griffin blasts up the middle on a simple quarterback draw. He notices the Rams in a "split-six" front with the defensive tackles shading the guards to the outside, leaving the middle wide open. He reads the weakness and exploits it for his second rushing touchdown.

While Griffin is 20 for 29 for 206 yards with a touchdown and a pick, Bradford quietly puts together a 300-yard, 3-touchdown game with no scripted touchdown celebrations. It's clear that Griffin is pop culture's quarterback, while Bradford toils in a nondescript media market for a starless team with very little national recognition. The game essentially ends on a stupid unsportsmanlike conduct penalty on Josh Morgan, who throws a ball at the face of the NFL's ultimate instigator, Cortland Finnegan. Washington goes down 31-28, but it does nothing to dampen Griffin-mania.

In a Week 4 matchup with Tampa Bay, Griffin was held out of the end zone through the air (though he amassed 323 yards), but was a key contributor in the run game, rushing for 43 and a score, while Alfred Morris emerged as a star, running for 113 yards and a score of his own.

More importantly, Griffin engineered the final drive in the final minute that led to a Billy Cundiff field goal, enabling the Redskins to end a 2-game skid by winning 24-22. And Griffin got a chance to call his own plays, as his in-helmet headset gave out. "In practice every week, we always practice me calling plays in two-minute, acting as if the headset goes out," Griffin told reporters. "I had to call a couple of my own plays, and we moved the chains and got in field-goal range. It was very neat how that practice situation, that practice scenario, actually played out in the game."[1] Griffin completed four passes on the drive and had a key 15-yard scramble to put his team into position to win.

"You take a look at the last two games, and we found a way to not win them, and this one we found a way to win it," said Mike Shanahan after the game.[2]

————

In Week 5 of the NFL season, Griffin and the Redskins play host to the Atlanta Falcons and Matt Ryan, himself a former number one draft choice. Ryan has matured into one of the better quarterbacks in pro football, seeming to shape himself in the Brees/Brady/Manning mold of PhD-level quarterbacking—steeped in pocket presence, sound decision-making, and the ability to make every throw to a cadre of talented young receivers, including Roddy White and 2011 first-rounder Julio Jones.

Today Ryan is carving up the Redskins defense, making frequent use of thirty-seven-year-old tight end Tony Gonzalez, who seems to catch every ball thrown his way. The young Redskin linebacking corps (Fletcher notwithstanding) doesn't seem to have an answer for him, and Ryan's only gaffe comes on a swing pass that is knocked down and intercepted by athletic second-year OLB Ryan Kerrigan, who takes the ball all the way back for a touchdown.

Offensively, the Redskins rely heavily on a steady dose of young running back Alfred Morris, who has been a revelation for the young team.

To say that sixth-round draft choice Alfred Morris was unheralded would be a massive understatement. He has a name and a jersey number reminiscent of a 1980s back (Alfred Anderson, Vikings), and when he arrived in Washington, he had a depth chart full of backs that he needed to beat out for significant playing time. Ahead of Morris were Roy Helu Jr.—he of the Nebraska pedigree; Evan Royster, who starred at Penn State; and productive NFL journeyman Tim Hightower.

Out of high school, Morris considered walking on at West Virginia, who recruited him as a linebacker. His mother encouraged him to pray about it, and instead he chose to accept the one scholarship offer he received, signing with Florida Atlantic. There he played for old-school coaching legend Howard Schnellenberger, going 1-11 (0-8 in the Sun Belt Conference) his senior season. Highly touted, he wasn't. Morris isn't especially huge at 5 feet 10 inches, 218 pounds, nor does he look especially fast. What he is, however, is an instinctive, one-cut back in the mold of other unheralded backs (like Terrell Davis, Olandis Gary, and Mike Anderson) whom Mike Shanahan made famous in Denver.

"He's definitely been a surprise story—not only for the media, but for the players as well," said Griffin in an NFL.com piece. "It's been great to watch him go out there and work. He's truly something special."[3]

Through Week 6, Morris leads all rookies in rushing and is sixth in the NFL with 538 yards rushing. Griffin and Morris have 927 yards between them, eclipsing the rushing totals of twenty-nine NFL teams.

"He has a great attitude about himself," said veteran middle linebacker London Fletcher, whose locker resides between that of Griffin and Morris. "He doesn't get caught up in a whole lot of [stuff] that a lot of rookies get caught up in. He just wants to work."[4]

Morris drives a silver Mazda with 125,000 miles on it: a vehicle that stands in stark contrast to the shiny, almost-obligatory SUVs that now dominate NFL parking lots. It is a gesture that seems to say, "I remember where I came from," while also saying, "I know that this may not last forever."[5] Morris seems, above all, thankful for the opportunity he's been given.

Today he is gashing the Falcons, primarily between the tackles, and he shows a keen ability to make the right one-cut at the perfect time and place. Midway through the third quarter, as the Redskins enter the red zone, he has 14 carries for 106 yards.

The Redskins enter the game a perfect 8 for 8 in goal-to-go situations and find themselves in a third and goal near the end of the quarter, with the game knotted at 7. Griffin is a marked man in these situations, as he has 4 rushing touchdowns already on the season. He is lined up in a shotgun formation, with Morris at his side; and after receiving the snap and finding his receivers covered, he rolls to his right. He is pursued by defensive tackle Jonathan Babineaux, but when he tries to slide, 250-pound Falcons linebacker Sean Weatherspoon approaches like a rocket and launches his shoulder into the side of Griffin's helmet, causing his head to ricochet to the side. Griffin's body lands facedown, prone on the turf for an extended moment. All of the air seems to leave FedExField as the team awaits the training staff.

The play is shown, repeatedly, from different angles. It is violence, largely, that sells, but it's also violence (and brain injury) that has former players involved in class-action lawsuits with the league and has the league enacting new concussion legislation to prevent players from reentering games prematurely. This, however, will be hard to police. Chicago Bears veteran linebacker Brian Urlacher was quoted in a *New York Times* piece as saying that he would "fake it" ("it" being health, ostensibly) to return to action sooner. He later said, "I don't know how you can lie these days with all the [stuff] they have to see who's concussed and who's not. I don't know how they can tell in the first place. I think the helmets aren't very good. I wear an old helmet and Lance

[Briggs] wears an old helmet. We don't get concussed. We have some pretty good collisions, [but] we don't get concussed. I think a lot of it has to do with the helmets. They're saying they're better but they must not be because people are getting more concussions now."[6]

With Griffin's first pro concussion, the sand begins trickling through the hourglass on the rest of his career. He was knocked out of the Texas Tech game with a concussion in 2011 as well. As the NFL becomes more stringent with its concussion legislation, there are players—like Detroit running back Jahvid Best—who may never play again due to multiple head injuries.

Late in the 2011 season, the league sent a memo to each team detailing its new concussion policy, in which a non-team-employee would be on hand with the express purpose of diagnosing concussions.

"First, we have arranged for a certified athletic trainer to be at each game to monitor play of both teams and provide medical staffs with any relevant information that may assist them in determining the most appropriate evaluation and treatment," the memo reads. "This athletic trainer will be stationed in a booth upstairs with access to video replay and direct communication to the medical staffs of both teams. In most cases, the athletic trainer will be affiliated with a major college program in the area or will have previously been affiliated with an NFL club."[7]

The memo says that this trainer will *not* "diagnose or prescribe treatment, nor have any authority to direct that a player be removed from the game . . . [and the trainer will] provide information to team medical staffs" should team staff miss a potential concussion or injury amid play.[8]

This is largely immaterial when the FedExField crowd chants, "RG! RG!" as Griffin rises to his feet and removes his headgear, revealing the trademark braids. He will not return, and will join the ranks of NFL starting quarterbacks who have missed significant time with concussions this season, including Alex Smith, Jay Cutler, Matt Cassel, and Mike Vick. It is a reminder of the precarious, often unprotected state of the running quarterback.

———

On another field, many miles away, South Carolina running back Marcus Lattimore is a living, breathing, feel-good story. Lattimore was a high school player of the year in 2008 and a *USA Today* All-American selection as a high school senior in 2009 at Byrnes High School in Duncan, South Carolina.

In just his second career college game, Lattimore hung 182 rushing yards on the mighty Georgia Bulldogs and broke 42 tackles in the process. He appeared to be the perfect blend of size, speed, and strength (at 6 feet tall and 232 pounds), and seemed destined to cement himself as the most decorated running back in South Carolina's history (no disrespect to George Rogers). Lattimore quickly achieved local hero status by spurning the Auburn Tigers in order to stay in his home state.

After his freshman season, Lattimore was named a second-team All-American selection, as well as the *Sporting News* freshman of the year. He started his sophomore season just as hot, rushing for 176 yards against Georgia and setting a school-record 246 against Navy. He would tear a knee ligament on October 15 against the Mississippi State Bulldogs and be declared out for the remainder of the season. It was a blow to South Carolina fans, as well as to the future prospects of Lattimore, who seemed to be on course for an Adrian Peterson–esque college career.

Still, the player defied all odds, rehabbed his injury after surgery, and took the field in 2012. In his first game back after the injury, Lattimore rushed for over 100 yards and a pair of touchdowns against Vanderbilt and appeared to have regained, if not all of his pre-injury form, enough to cement himself as an above-average SEC tailback with a bright pro future ahead. What's more, Lattimore is reported to be an all-around great kid who excels in the classroom and off the field.

Against Tennessee on October 27, 2012, Lattimore took a routine handoff in the second quarter and moved to his left through the line of scrimmage. He was held up from behind briefly while a Tennessee defender launched himself at Lattimore's lower body, causing his knee to bend and contort at a grotesque angle. After the play, Lattimore sat up for a moment, seeming to survey his knee with a look of horror on his face. As SC trainers raced to the field, they encouraged him to remain on his back, primarily so that he wouldn't have to see his own leg.

The injury is reminiscent of Los Angeles Raiders running back Napoleon McCallum's injury in 1994 against San Francisco, when he was spun down awkwardly by linebacker Ken Norton, shearing every ligament in his knee and rupturing an artery in the process. McCallum would never play again.

"Honestly, I thought I was dreaming," said Lattimore of the injury in a later interview during South Carolina's bowl game. "I thought I would wake up from the dream . . . I went into shock and seen [sic] how my leg was awkwardly looking."[9]

"I've known this kid since high school," said former NFL coach and ESPN analyst Jon Gruden, "and I can honestly say that everyone who comes in contact with this kid is a better person for it."[10]

CBS Sports reported that Lattimore's injury is similar to the one suffered by former Miami Hurricanes (and current Denver Bronco) running back Willis McGahee in the 2003 Fiesta Bowl, in which he tore his ACL, MCL, and PCL. After a year hiatus and an aggressive marketing campaign by agent Drew Rosenhaus, McGahee was still drafted in the first round and is still enjoying a solid NFL career. It is his story that gives Lattimore and his fans hope in the wake of this injury.

As the training staff attends to Lattimore—even pulling him to his feet—members of the UT Volunteers and USC Gamecocks gather around their wounded teammate. Even a few Tennessee players are crying. In a moment, it is a picture of both what is grotesque about football (man's fallibility, brokenness) and also what can be great about it, as boys momentarily stop being warriors and resume being human.

Lattimore's injury sparked an outcry of response from players all over the country, with Robert Griffin leading the way. He tweeted, "We are warriors on the field, but are humans as well. I pray everyone sends prayers forth for Marcus Lattimore & others that are injured."[11]

———

On the sideline at FedExField, Robert Griffin receives treatment for a cut on the inside of his lip and appears to be receiving testing and treatment for a concussion. Behind him, his backup quarterback Kirk Cousins is taking warm-up throws. Shanahan and the Redskins were roundly criticized for taking a second quarterback in the fourth round of the 2012 draft. Now it looks like, if not a stroke of genius, at least a bit of forethought. The thought is that if one is staking one's hopes on a running quarterback, that running quarterback had better come with an insurance policy.

On a gray afternoon in Landover, Maryland, as Robert Griffin ducks into a small door leading underneath the stadium, Kirk Cousins bro-hugs Kyle Shanahan and takes the field for his first significant action as a professional.

His first professional pass is a 4-yard hitch to Josh Morgan. On third down he's welcomed to the NFL by veteran defensive end John Abraham, who speed rushes around tackle Tyler Polumbus to hit Cousins's arm as he throws. Atlanta is loading the box, shutting down Alfred Morris, and daring the rookie quarterback to beat them.

On third down in his second series as a pro, Cousins strikes. Under pressure from the Falcon front four, he drifts back into the pocket and finds veteran receiver Santana Moss streaking, uncovered, past the middle of the Atlanta secondary. Cousins puts the ball on the money, and Moss dances into the end zone untouched, giving the Redskins new life and a 17-14 lead.

The play is an example of the oddity of NFL life—an untested rookie throwing to a grown man. Moss, formerly a star at the University of Miami (FL), has starred with the New York Jets and is now on the downside of his career with Washington. He has gone from flashy, blingy, cornrowed Miami sensation to sensible, veteran role player who knows he needs to keep grinding to stay relevant in the league. Moss has seen his role diminish with the acquisition of Pierre Garçon, but he is still a valuable third-down target for his rookie quarterbacks.

A late field goal and Michael Turner touchdown run put Atlanta up 24-17, and Cousins takes the field again with just over two minutes remaining. He hits Garçon for 20, then Moss in the flat for 3. His next ball, a deep out intended for tight end Fred Davis, is thrown into double coverage and is picked by veteran cornerback Dunta Robinson.

Cousins takes over again with 1:21 remaining, having gone 5-8 for 111 yards, a TD, and a pick. Cousins lines up in a shotgun formation, with three-wides, and is hit as he throws again, looking for Santana Moss deep. He is picked by safety Thomas DeCoud, who seals the win for Atlanta. Gonzales, the veteran, finishes with 13 catches for 122 yards in victory, helping the Falcons to an unblemished 5-0 start, the first in franchise history.

The player who put Griffin out of the game, Weatherspoon, dances on the sideline with the story of the moment, DeCoud. As Robert Griffin is examined beneath the stadium and Cousins walks off the field in what has become a driving rainstorm, the Redskins fall to 2-3 (losers of 8 straight at home) and seemingly have more questions than answers.

FIGHT FOR OLD DIXIE: A BRIEF RACIAL HISTORY OF THE WASHINGTON REDSKINS

It's Week 6 of the NFL season, and the Washington Redskins play host to the Minnesota Vikings, who bring a promising second-year quarterback in Christian Ponder, a defense led by aging sackmaster Jared Allen, and a rejuvenated Adrian Peterson, who tore his ACL and MCL less than a year ago on this selfsame FedExField turf.

Coming into the game, Griffin leads the entire league in completion percentage, hitting on an astonishing 69.1 percent of his passes—which is partly a testament to his own accuracy and partly to Kyle Shanahan's shrewd and efficient play calling. Shanahan has called short passes and utilized play-action passes as Washington's run game—led in part by Griffin—has made defenses commit more defenders in the box.

Concussed a week ago versus the Falcons, Griffin claims to be "free of all symptoms" and is in uniform and cleared to play. He's not only cleared to play; he has 63 rushing yards and has taken numerous hits by the time the Redskins are trying to salt away the game in the fourth quarter. And his rushing yards—the majority of them anyway—have come on designed runs, meaning that Griffin isn't just breaking the pocket and scrambling. The team is treating him like another running back, often sending him between the tackles like they would Alfred Morris. It's a risky strategy designed to take advantage of Griffin's prodigious gifts, but also a strategy that figures to take weeks, and maybe years, off his football life.

"When Robert gets in top gear, it's like watching a track meet," said Santana Moss afterward. "And he ain't coming in second."[1]

With 2:56 remaining until the Redskins secure their first home victory in eight long games, Griffin approaches the line of scrimmage. After receiving the snap, he is flushed from the pocket, breaking to his left. Unlike the designed runs before, this play is an unplanned scramble that sends him to the second level of the Vikings defense. There, he simply uses long strides and track speed to outrace safety Harrison Smith—who has an angle—76 yards into the end zone as the crowd chants, "RG3! RG3!" at an ear-splitting decibel. Tight ends coach Sean McVay later told Griffin that he felt a "gust of wind" as Griffin sped by him. "I took off running and got to the sideline, thought about running out of bounds—because everyone's been telling me that lately," Griffin later told the media with a big smile. "I felt like I had the guy outflanked, and then I just took off running. And the rest is history."[2]

When he finishes the run, Griffin glides into the back of the end zone and leaps, Lambeau-style, into the waiting arms of a group of ecstatic Redskins fans—the two grabbiest of whom happen to be young white women. The camera lingers.

———

The Washington Redskins were the last NFL team to integrate, doing so in 1962 when they were threatened by Secretary of the Interior Stewart L. Udall. Referring to the Redskins as the "Paleskins," Udall let owner George Preston Marshall know that unless the Redskins signed a black player, they would no longer have use of D.C. Stadium, which happened to be publicly financed and managed by the parks system.

The 1960 Redskins were dreadful at 1-9-2, and by the mid-1950s, they were the only team in the NFL without a black player. At the close of 1960, there was an average of six black players per team, and many more in the rival American Football League.

George Preston Marshall, Washington's owner, was savaged in the local press for his "white supremacist policies" that were meant to appease a predominantly Southern radio and television audience. For many years the Redskins were the NFL's southernmost franchise; and to that point, the Redskins had passed on drafting such black stars as Jim Brown, Jim Parker, Roosevelt Grier, Roosevelt Brown, and Bobby Mitchell, just to name a few. In the 1960 draft alone, they shunned Elijah Pitts and Irv Cross, opting instead to draft Wake Forest quarterback Norm Snead along with seven other white players. Wrote Tex Maule in *Sports Illustrated*, "Snead faces the blackest future and the whitest huddle in the league."[3]

We live in an era of rampant media overcoverage of everything—from the fact that Robert Griffin III has the Redskins in playoff contention, to the fact that Robert Griffin III allegedly bought a brand-new Bentley for his white fiancée, as reported in a headline by BlackSportsOnline.[4] Perhaps more than any other single item, the kind of scrutiny that Griffin lives with (the car he bought his girl) has given me great sympathy for him. Not surprisingly, he has become an object of fascination, hope, and in some cases disappointment for the black community.

ESPN analyst Rob Parker—albeit an "analyst" for one of ESPN's third- or fourth-tier, sportswriters-screaming-at-each-other daytime programs—raised the question, "Is [RG3] a brother, or is he a cornball brother?" To which his cohosts asked the obvious and helpful question, "What does that mean?" Parker then went on to explain that a "cornball brother" is, "He's black . . . but he's not really down with the cause. He's not one of us."[5]

Note: Have these shows ever brought you even a modicum of joy, happiness, or insight when it comes to your sport or team? Does the existence of these shows, droning on day after day after day, suck some of the joy out of football—the joy that used to come with waiting a week to see your stars on television? I used to love seeing Walter Payton play on a Sunday afternoon, knowing I would basically have to wait an entire week to see him again. I miss this. Also, I'm getting too old for all of this, I think, because I simply don't care what kind of car Robert Griffin III buys for his girl.

Caveat: I'm white and therefore will never fully understand the importance and nuance of a discussion like this, but I'm going to make my best effort anyway.

Parker went on to say in his segment—which, by the way, quickly devolved into the kind of situation in which you're literally cringing in embarrassment for the person who's speaking, hopeful that they will see the error in their ways and shut up as soon as possible—that "he's not one of us. He's kind of black, but he's not really, like, the guy you want to hang out with. . . . I keep hearing these things. We all know he has a white fiancée and there's all this talk about, he's a Republican, which there's no information at all. I'm just trying to dig deeper into why he has an issue."[6]

I'm just trying to understand Parker's logic here and trying to define what it means to "have an issue." Apparently, to Parker, having a white fiancée and allegedly (albeit with no "information") being a Republican constitute "having an issue" and not being "loyal to the cause." Also, if I'm understanding Parker correctly, being the kind of guy that Parker wants to "hang out with" means not having "an issue."

These are strange times indeed.

———

In 1962, amid protests from fans and pressure from the Kennedy Administration, the Washington Redskins signed black halfback Bobby Mitchell to a $20,000 contract—at that point the richest in team history. In the opening game of the 1962 season at Dallas, Mitchell ran a kickoff back 92 yards for a score and caught 2 touchdown passes. The Redskins opened the season 4-0-2. They would never again refuse to draft or sign black players. A four-time Pro Bowler, Mitchell was inducted into the Hall of Fame in 1983.

Ironically, the team that had excluded black players for decades won the first Super Bowl quarterbacked by a black player. In January 1988, led by Doug Williams and running back Timmy Smith, the Redskins dominated the Denver Broncos in a 42-10 blowout, forever putting to rest the ridiculous notion that black quarterbacks didn't have the intellectual makeup for on-field leadership.[7] Williams had the hopes and dreams of an entire race on his broad shoulders that afternoon as the game became much more than a game. At media day, before the game, Williams was asked, "How long have you been a black quarterback?"

"They didn't call me and say, 'We're signing you for Black America,'" Williams explained when he signed with Washington. "They said, 'We're signing you for the Washington Redskins.'"[8]

———

Griffin may or may not be a Republican, and ultimately it doesn't matter, but I do know that he has deftly sidestepped the political question in much the same way that Michael Jordan did. Michael Jordan's "cause" was always Michael Jordan, and there was an odd sort of purity in that. There was a simplicity in knowing Jordan was always looking out for the best interests of Jordan, that he wasn't trying to be a symbol for anything, and that he wasn't throwing his support behind either political candidate.

At one point in the aforementioned ESPN analysis-gone-wrong, cohost Skip Bayless asked, with a straight face, "What do RG3's braids say to you?" Seriously, I couldn't make this stuff up. To which Parker replied, "To me that's very urban. . . . Wearing braids is . . . you're a brother. You're a brother if you've got braids."

To which Stephen A. Smith (also African American, also super entertaining, and in my opinion the king of Daytime Talking Heads) replied, "I'm uncomfortable with where we just went." You know it's gotten bad when a personality like Stephen A. Smith is the calm voice of reason.

I *knew* the "How Black Is Robert Griffin?" story would surface. Knew it. I would have bet the contents of my bank account on it, because it surfaced with guys like Tiger Woods (didn't want race to define him, was decried for "acting white"), Allen Iverson (probably the least white-acting black athlete in the history of black athletes), and Mike Vick.

Griffin's father, RG2, was vocal in support of his son, telling *USA Today* that he was "baffled" by Parker's comments. "He needs to define what 'one of us' is," he said. "I wouldn't say it's racism. I would just say some people put things out there about people so they can stir things up."[9]

Stirring things up, it seems, is what ratings are made of. ESPN released a statement saying that Parker's comments were "inappropriate," and that they are "evaluating" what to do next. To his credit, he publicly apologized to Griffin for the comments. Either way, if Parker is fired, ESPN can pick from an almost limitless supply of bombastic talking heads who are willing to say anything for fifteen minutes of fame. Parker's greatest mistake in all of this was believing that he mattered to ESPN or the viewing and listening public. Much like the athletes he covers, he is completely disposable and expendable. For a day he was useful for a ratings and publicity spike. Tomorrow he will be discarded. Or, if they choose to do nothing, the story will more than likely go away and be replaced by something different and more sensational tomorrow. Even Griffin's Heisman Trophy win has taken on a transitory feel, as he was succeeded in Heisman victory by an equally sensational player (Johnny Manziel), who plays the same position, comes from the same state (Texas), and is a freshman to boot (making him historical).

The fact of the matter is that Robert Griffin III is walking a *very* fine line that includes the expectations of his team, his fan base, Madison Avenue, and black America. Griffin, essentially, needs to be "black enough" to pacify the people who want or need him to be black, but "white enough" to not alienate the legions of white people who are happy to buy Adidas shoes, season ticket packages, and Subway sandwiches from a black athlete whose braids really aren't all that intimidating because of what a good kid he seems to be. In the midst of all of this, he has to lead his teammates, watch film, memorize a playbook, read defenses, play through pain, and maintain relationships.

We are in awe of his talent and envious of his opportunities. But for the first time, do we feel sorry for Robert Griffin III?

9

A GROWN MAN'S GAME: ROBERT GRIFFIN III IS HUMAN

I t's definitely a grown man's game," said Robert Griffin in an interview with ESPN's Erin Andrews during the Redskins bye-week. "The players are bigger . . . everybody's got an All-American on their roster."[1]

Losses to the Pittsburgh Steelers and Cam Newton's Carolina Panthers represented Griffin's toughest and most frustrating games as a professional. The games were both blueprints for future defenses in terms of bottling Griffin's playmaking ability, and proof of his uncommon poise and leadership, even in the face of adversity.

"Like we talked about at the beginning of the year, the more of a balanced attack you have, the less pressure you put on a quarterback," said Mike Shanahan before the Pittsburgh game. "You don't like to throw too much on a quarterback because he hasn't experienced everything. Robert picks things up very quickly. He's a threat both in the run and the pass so the defense has to play fairly honest. He learns very quickly. He knows that you can't win football games if you turn the football over and he has done a great job throughout the preseason and the regular season trying to avoid that."[2]

"My goal is to make sure I'm the starting quarterback for this team for a long time . . . and it is pressure," Griffin told Andrews. "More pressure than I've had to deal with in my life. If there's no pressure on you, you have no opportunity to get a diamond."[3]

The line is becoming something of a brand-builder for Griffin, who is now ranking near the top of a list of starting quarterbacks in the National Football League—a list that is, arguably, deeper and more top-loaded with quality than it's ever been. There are truly only a handful of teams that are unhappy with their starters. I ranked each NFL starter (in Week 8) and divided them into tiers below for the purpose of illustrating both the depth of quality competition at the quarterback position and also putting into perspective Griffin's early success.[*]

THE HALL OF FAME TIER

Tom Brady, Patriots. Everybody in this tier has won at least one Super Bowl, and Brady is at the top of this list because Brady is the total package. He has Super Bowl wins, mad statistical output, and has piloted one of the steadiest franchises in football for a decade.

Drew Brees, Saints. Brees, like Brady, is an absolute surgeon in the pocket and has the ability to eviscerate any defense that gives him time to throw. The mark of a great quarterback is that he can make average receivers look outstanding, which is all the more apparent when those average receivers go to play in different offenses and then look average again.

---

[*]   These rankings appear revised for the postseason in Appendix A on page 165.

Aaron Rodgers, Packers. If you had told Packer fans, "Someone will come along and make you at least momentarily forget about Brett Favre," they would have been incredulous. If the Packers can find a running game (and maybe even if they don't), he will be very good for a very long time.

Peyton Manning, Broncos. Manning's receivers this season are Eric Decker, Brandon Stokely (who's thirty-seven), and Demaryius Thomas. That said, Peyton Manning is very, very good; and the Broncos absolutely made the right decision when they cut bait on Tebow, a fan and media darling, and brought in a Hall of Famer with fuel left in the tank.

Ben Roethlisberger, Steelers. Some will argue with Roethlisberger's inclusion in the Hall of Fame tier, but I think he belongs here because (a) he's won two Super Bowls and (b) he probably does more pure quarterbacking each week than anyone else on this list. By pure quarterbacking, I mean that he's keeping plays alive with his feet, utilizing the pocket, and making insanely good throws while also managing the game.

THE "NOT QUITE ELITE BUT STILL VERY GOOD" TIER

Eli Manning, Giants. The obvious response to Roethlisberger's inclusion above is to say, "Eli has also won two Super Bowls, so why isn't he in the Hall of Fame tier?" It's a fair question, but while he's played on great Giants teams and played very well at his position, I'm not convinced that he's as good as the quarterbacks above him on the list.

Matt Ryan, Falcons. Ryan has all the makings of a "face of the franchise" quarterback. He's not surly or truculent like Cutler, he makes wise decisions with the football, and he has an elite pair of receivers in Roddy White and Julio Jones to whom to throw the football.

Matthew Stafford, Lions. Stafford has elite arm talent, guts, and above-average charisma; and given the fact that a full half of his team (Suh, Titus Young, et al.) and his coach (Jim Schwartz) are completely out of control and will probably be gone soon, Stafford is doing a more than adequate job of holding the fort and making something out of nothing.

Jay Cutler, Bears. My main issue with ranking Cutler this high is the sneaking feeling that in a year or two, or even by the end of this season, he will have found a way to burn his bridge in Chicago and/or he will have been leapfrogged on this list by both Andrew Luck and Robert Griffin (and maybe Russell Wilson).

THE "OUTSTANDING ROOKIES WITH CRAZY UPSIDE" TIER

Andrew Luck, Colts. Luck looks like Peyton Manning 2.0 in terms of the way he moves in the pocket and reads defenses. He has the arm talent to spin the ball downfield, he's getting a ton out of a very limited roster, and he's making the Colts look like geniuses for letting Manning go, even though Manning still had a lot in the tank.

Robert Griffin III, Redskins. Griffin is lighting up defenses with his zone-read planned runs and the subsequent play-action game that is possible as a result of those runs. Alfred Morris has been a revelation in Mike Shanahan's zone scheme, and the sky seems to be the limit for Griffin, who is scarily accurate and wise with the football for a young player. It's not a stretch to say that the Redskins may have their most talented quarterback since Sammy Baugh.

THE "NOT QUITE ELITE BUT STILL VERY GOOD" SECOND-TIER

Matt Schaub, Texans. If someone put a gun to your head and said, "You can start a team and you have to pick either Matt Schaub or Jay Culter to play quarterback," you would probably pick Cutler for his arm and athleticism, but you should probably pick Schaub instead.

Joe Flacco, Ravens. As "Game Managers" go, Flacco is one of the best in the business.

Andy Dalton, Bengals. Dalton's head coach, Marvin Lewis, shows a preternatural ability to do just enough to not get fired, year in and year out. That said, the acquisition of Dalton and A. J. Green may buy him a few more years.

Philip Rivers, Chargers. Rivers was drafted alongside Eli Manning; and while thought of as elite, and while engaging in some high-profile yap-fests with both Jay Cutler and Peyton Manning, he has failed to even play in a Super Bowl, much less win one.

THE "YOUNG GUYS WITH FRANCHISE-TYPE UPSIDE BUT SIGNIFICANT QUESTION MARKS" TIER

Cam Newton, Panthers. In year two, Cam Newton is learning the hard way what it means to be a star player on a horrible, going-nowhere team. Does Newton have the mental and emotional intelligence to be able to navigate these waters graciously? His megawatt smile made frequent appearances when he was putting up PlayStation numbers last year, but he's been surly and openly unhappy this year.

Josh Freeman, Bucs. Freeman lost weight this offseason and is subsequently moving much better in the pocket. It doesn't hurt to have a superfreak rookie at tailback in Doug Martin and a pair of extremely legit and extremely big playmakers at wideout in Vincent Jackson and Mike Williams.

Sam Bradford, Rams. He's plateaued a bit after a very encouraging rookie campaign, but does Bradford's plateau have more to do with the fact that he plays for one of the most consistently bad franchises in the NFL over the last ten years?

Jake Locker, Titans. His coach described him as a passing quarterback who can run, and it's an apt description of the athletic Locker. He seems, more importantly, to have the mental makeup of a solid starter and a franchise leader.

THE "TONY ROMO" TIER

Tony Romo, Cowboys. Tony Romo gets his own tier because he's no longer a young guy with upside, nor is he necessarily ready to be put out to pasture by the Dallas brass. He's shown flashes of the old, gunslinging Romo at times, and he's been awful at times, primarily when he's trying to do too much with an underachieving team around him.

THE "WE'RE DISSATISFIED BUT NOT QUITE READY TO MAKE A MOVE" TIER

Mark Sanchez, Jets. Sanchez led the Jets to two straight AFC Championship appearances, but that was when he had a better running game (Thomas Jones, anyone?), better receivers (Santonio Holmes, Jerricho Cotchery), and a better defense (a pre-ridiculous, pre-decline Bart Scott) around him.

Alex Smith, 49ers. Smith has had a long and winding career since being the number one overall pick out of Utah. He's played for several coaches and seems to be playing stable, productive, consistent football under Jim Harbaugh.

THE "WE'VE INVESTED IN YOUNG GUYS WITH UPSIDE WHO HAVEN'T ALWAYS PERFORMED GREAT BUT WE'RE STILL HOPEFUL" TIER

Ryan Tannehill, Dolphins. Tannehill has all the physical tools in the world but is operating with a franchise left tackle who's having the worst season of his career (Jake Long), an overrated running back (Reggie Bush), and a variety of receivers for whom the "unremarkable" label might be charitable.

Russell Wilson, Seahawks. Sometimes electrifying, sometimes frustrating, always undersized, Wilson wrested the job away from big-dollar free agent Matt Flynn and has held on to it ever since. He's ranked ahead of Ponder because he's actually won games on his own.

Christian Ponder, Vikings. It remains to be seen whether Ponder will ever develop into more than a game manager, although being a game manager with Adrian Peterson in your backfield and Percy Harvin on the wing isn't a bad gig.

Brandon Weeden, Browns. Weeden has had a few good, not great, games for Cleveland, and he's had some very bad games as well.

THE "FREE AGENCY AND DRAFT CAN'T COME SOON ENOUGH" TIER

Carson Palmer, Raiders. Palmer gets placement at the top of this list because of his past achievement and reputation, but Oakland will probably go in a different direction after another dreadful season.

Blaine Gabbert, Jaguars. Gabbert put up huge numbers in a gimmicky college offense and had great pre-draft workouts. Thus, he was probably overdrafted by a franchise that was desperate to fill seats and sell jerseys, for which they should have just gone ahead and drafted Tim Tebow.

Ryan Fitzpatrick, Bills. The three interesting things about Fitzpatrick are that he went to Harvard, that he has a great beard, and that he beat out Vince Young to hang on to the starting job in the offseason.

Mike Vick, Eagles. When Vick was released from prison, hopes and anticipation ran high. But let's be honest for a second: Mike Vick was never a great passer; he never developed the ability to read the whole field and consistently carve up defenses with his arm. He also never showed the ability to stay healthy for an entire season. For Vick, 2010 is looking more like a statistical aberration than the norm.

Matt Cassel, Chiefs. Cassel wasn't a starter at USC; he was Tom Brady's backup in New England and earned his big contract and starting shot in Kansas City as a result of his relationship with Scott Pioli and a few great games driving the Ferrari Testarossa that is the Patriots offense.

Kevin Kolb and John Skelton and Ryan Lindley, Cardinals. Final Jeopardy answer: Who are three players who have failed to look good even when throwing to Larry Fitzgerald and Michael Floyd?

With the exception of the bottom tier, this is a pretty solid list, with five or six locks for the Hall of Fame and lots of guys who have shown they have the potential to be very good, if not potential Hall of Famers themselves. Even the middle-to-bottom tier has some promise (Tannehill, Weeden) and some big names (Carson Palmer).

———

It's a cold, rainy afternoon in Pittsburgh, which is fitting for the occasion and the kind of team Pittsburgh routinely fields—tough, physical, veteran laden, and relatively mistake free. Their objective will be to rein in one of the NFL's rookie sensations, a point of pride for the Steelers defense and their elite, ageless coordinator Dick LeBeau.

"They love to blitz quarterbacks, period," said Griffin in the week leading up to the game. "They like to bring a lot of pressure and make it a chaotic game. It's something that you truly can't be ready for until you're out there on the field—definitely watching tape and being ready for their blitzes. If they don't blitz and decide to drop into coverage, that won't shock us either because we've seen about everything that a team can do. They run that 3-4 defense and that's similar to the one we run. They've had guys that have been in that system for a long time so they know what they're doing. I look forward to playing them. It'll be a good chess match."[4]

As poised as he's been on the field, Griffin has become an adept manager of the media in these settings as well. In the same session, he's asked about what he's learned from Roethlisberger (not much), if he's excited about the return of previously released tight end Chris Cooley (yes), worried about not having Pierre Garçon and Fred Davis in the lineup (not really), worried about his off-field commitments encroaching on his football time (no), happy for backup tight end Logan Paulsen's opportunities (yes), and pressured by the success Roethlisberger achieved as a rookie (no).[5] Griffin is quickly and easily learning the art of talking a lot while actually saying very little. It's not so much *what* he says, though, as much as *how* he says it. He's always positive, always makes eye contact, and rarely sulks (like Newton).

"It's big. Body language is a big tell-all," he explained. "For football players, you don't want to get way too excited after a win and be holly-jolly and then be super down after a loss. You stay even keeled—let guys know you feel like you're doing the right things as a team and eventually, those wins are going to start coming. You just stay at it. You're not lackadaisical about it all. You do have a sense of urgency but you're not panicking."[6]

Across the field, Roethlisberger is something of a modern gold-standard for young quarterbacks, winning a division championship in his first year and a Super Bowl in his second. He's also an example of a quarterback who freelances, keeps plays alive with his feet, leaves the pocket frequently, and also pays a punishing physical price as he's only started all 16 games in a season once in his career (2008).

The Steelers come out of the locker room sporting a set of horrific, jailhouse-meets-bumblebee 1934 throwback uniforms. The NFL's alternate-jersey obsession seems to truly know no bounds as it dares to mess with the regular Steeler uniform, one of the simplest and best in pro sports. Defensive coordinator Dick LeBeau is an impressive 14-1 when coaching against rookie quarterbacks, but admitted that the "[meeting] room got silent" when watching RG3 film during the week. Before the game, NBA legend LeBron James Tweeted, "RG III is a monster."[7]

"He's a special talent—not only in terms of what he can do with his arms, but also his legs," said Steelers coach Mike Tomlin during the week. "I really think they're doing a nice job of maximizing his talents and putting him in a position to be successful. But bigger than the physical talent, it's obvious that the stage isn't too big for him and he's really representing himself well and appears to be extremely comfortable while executing."[8]

The Steelers opened the game with a long, sustained drive against Jim Haslett's 3-4 defense—the same strategy employed by LeBeau, who is just employing his with much better personnel. The Redskins' leading sack man coming into the contest is outside linebacker Ryan Kerrigan, who has only 3.5. All told, the drive eats up 12 plays and seven minutes, proving that one way to slow RG3 down is simply to keep him off the field. Washington's linebackers, including London Fletcher making his 232nd career start, are playing deep—6 to 7 yards off the line of scrimmage—and are getting gashed downhill by big Steelers running back Jonathan Dwyer (nicknamed "The Minivan"). Roethlisberger tosses a short touchdown pass to third-string tight end Leonard Pope, making it look easy.

Robert Griffin leads the NFL in completion percentage coming into the contest, hitting an astonishing 70 percent of his throws, with 7 touchdowns and only 3 picks. On the first series, though, he's bottled up as the Steelers fill gaps and pursue as well as any team in the league. It's difficult to run Shanahan's signature zone-stretch against a good, disciplined 3-4 defense. During the week, at least, Tomlin wouldn't cop to doing anything special to prepare for Griffin's option attack, saying, "More than anything, you have to build defenses that are sound—that are capable of standing up and forcing units, are squared away, you know who sets the edge, who turns things back, what is the proper engagement or pursuit angles. We tend to do that with all the defenses. More importantly than trying to figure out how to stop an option-like attack, we knock the dust off our rules and play to them."[9]

Since Dick LeBeau took over in 2004, the Steelers are first in the league in sacks with 355, and more importantly are first in points allowed, giving up only 17 per game on average. Still, Griffin leads the Redskins into the red zone in the first quarter, only to see the drive stall on consecutive drops by young receivers Leonard Hankerson and Dezmon Briscoe. It's a cold, wet day, but they're both catchable balls and plays that should be made by NFL receivers.

On a fourth and goal in the second quarter, Griffin hits Santana Moss on a drag for the touchdown, but Kai Forbath's extra point is blocked. Griffin was 5 for 8 on the drive for 57 yards, developing a rhythm for the first time. Perhaps the most interesting play of the game takes place with 4:17 remaining in the second quarter. The Redskins run a reverse pass, with Griffin leaking out of the backfield and running down the left side of the field while wide receiver Joshua Morgan throws across the field. The pass is intended for Griffin, who is flagged for offensive pass interference and then blown up by veteran safety Ryan Clark. It's a questionable call, and a questionable way to use your newly minted multimillion-dollar franchise quarterback.

After the series he sits dejected and alone on the Redskins sideline.

"It is very frustrating," Griffin said after the game. "You want to go out, be successful, execute plays and have everything work for you and then . . . you have a day like today when you have almost nothing work for you."[10]

The final stats tell part of the story of Pittsburgh's defensive efficiency. The Redskins only rushed for 86 yards as a team, lost the time of possession battle, and Griffin was held to a meager 8 yards on 6 carries. And he was good, but not great, through the air, going 16-34 for 177 yards and a score. Granted, he didn't get any help from his receivers who dropped several easily catchable balls; and the Steelers defense was clutch on third down, with the Redskins converting only 3 of 12 third-down opportunities.

"We didn't want to get too creative," said Steelers defensive end Brett Keisel after the game. "We just wanted to play the way we know how." Added linebacker Larry Foote, "He wasn't running all over the place. The front seven got challenged by Mike [Tomlin] all week and they delivered."[11]

What's telling is that in each of the Redskins' losses, Griffin has been outplayed by the quarterback across the field. Today Roethlisberger was a cool 24-33 for 222 yards and 3 scores. Against the Rams in Week 2, Griffin had 2 scoring runs and a 68-yard touchdown pass to Leonard Hankerson, but was outplayed by former number one overall pick Sam Bradford, who had 310 yards and 3 touchdowns in the win. It was a costly loss for the Redskins, who lost defensive end Adam Carriker and outside linebacker Brian Orakpo to injuries in the first quarter.

In their home opener in Week 3, the Redskins lost to Andy Dalton and the Cincinnati Bengals as Dalton picked apart a vulnerable Washington secondary, reeling from the loss of Orakpo and his pass rush. Perhaps more than any of the previous games, this one was an illustration of Griffin's physical vulnerability. He was sacked 3 times by Bengals defensive end Michael Johnson, who abused Washington tackle Jordan Black. In addition to the sacks (6 total), he seemed to take a beating each time he ran, taking an especially wicked shot from linebacker Rey Maualuga after a fourth-quarter scramble. Still, Griffin was effective on the ground, leading the team in rushing with 85 yards on only 12 carries (with a score). But at what long-term cost?

Griffin would face a similar test the following week, against Carolina's resident Superman, Cam Newton. He insists the comparisons to the athletic Newton don't bother him, saying, "We are both athletic quarterbacks so him, myself, Mike Vick, Aaron Rodgers, all these guys, and even Jay Cutler went out there and ran a little bit Monday night. Whenever you can move a little bit, you're going to get those comparisons. I try not to play too much into that or listen to much of that at all."[12]

The fact is, Newton was statistically sensational for the 6-10 Panthers in 2011, throwing for over 4,000 yards and scoring an incredible 14 touchdowns on the ground. In a way, Newton dispelled some of the trepidations regarding running quarterbacks, as he was consistent and durable throughout the course of the season.

This season he's struggled, though, leading a 1-7 team that didn't make the jump that many expected in Newton's sophomore campaign. Newton has struggled statistically himself, throwing only one multiple-touchdown game (2 TDs in Week 4 against Atlanta), throwing only 5 TDs versus 8 picks, and seeing tougher run defenses as well. Of greater concern is Newton's attitude. He's an emotional player, but many wonder if that emotion isn't manifesting itself as immaturity in year two. Newton is a player who won a national title at the junior college level and then won another national title at Auburn. It remains to be seen whether he has the mental makeup to deal with adversity.

Before he was drafted, reports surfaced about an "attitude of entitlement." And a new report, from Yahoo! Sports' "Shutdown Corner" blog, paints of picture of Newton as almost universally disliked at last year's Pro Bowl, refusing requests for autographs and "dissing" the godfather of NFL veterans, Ravens linebacker Ray Lewis.[13]

For his part, Griffin explained that he would rather be compared to Aaron Rodgers—a passing quarterback with mobility—than Newton, still perceived as a "running quarterback." That, among other things, may have angered the Carolina Panthers who were deemed the Redskins' "Homecoming" opponent, at least by *Gameday* magazine.

"I look on [the program] and it says *homecoming*. And I'm thinking to myself, like, this is the *National Football League*. Are you serious? *Homecoming?*" Panthers running back DeAngelo Williams said.

"It was the whole team. That was *definitely* motivating. I mean, you don't say you're gonna have a *homecoming* in the National Football League. I mean, you do it in college. It's [against] one of those teams that's just terrible. You don't book a good team for homecoming."[14]

The Redskins were dressed in their own throwback uniforms—albeit much more tasteful than Pittsburgh's—a 1937 rendition that featured a helmet laquer meant to look like old leather.

The motivation seemed to work for Williams, whose 30-yard touchdown run was his longest of the season. Even the typically surly Newton—who can usually be found sulking by himself underneath a white towel on the bench—seemed more joyful. Newton's 82-yard pass to converted Appalachian State quarterback Armanti Edwards was the highlight of an efficient 13 for 23 performance that included an additional 37 yards and a rushing touchdown.

Regarding Newton: There's something that is, quite frankly, *nasty* about his demeanor, facial expressions, and celebrations after successful plays. He routinely taunts opposing defenses and crowds, as he did after scoring on a 1-yard plunge in the third quarter after the long pass to Edwards. He pointed derisively at the Washington crowd and then performed his already played Superman touchdown celebration. He did it all with an obnoxious sneer on his face. Newton seems comfortable playing the black-hatted villain role. Perhaps it's just his personality. He makes Mike Vick seem staid and dignified by comparison. I think this, plus the fact that his team is bad, will keep a pretty low ceiling on Newton's marketability as an endorser in the future. Simply stated, he's hard to like, and people want to buy products from people they like.

"It's like a gun," Newton once told Jon Gruden. "I'm that. And my ammunition is the criticism that people put into words to describe who I really am. That's what I use. That's my fuel to keep getting better and better."[15]

On the field, especially as runners, Griffin and Newton both seem extremely relaxed and confident, like great boxers who make their craft look easy. In fact, Fox pregame analyst Jimmy Johnson said of Griffin, "As a rookie, it's amazing. . . . I haven't seen anything like this."[16] Johnson has seen a lot of great quarterbacks, including his own Troy Aikman, who struggled mightily as a rookie, completing only 52 percent of his passes and throwing 18 interceptions (against only 9 touchdowns). Indeed, there is genius in both Griffin's ability and in the way he's deployed.

Griffin would have 215 passing yards and another 53 on the ground, but was held out of the end zone in both categories. Perhaps the most significant series came with five minutes remaining in the first half, when Carolina's defense shut down an Alfred Morris run and a swing pass to Brandon Banks, and then perfectly diagnosed and strung out a Robert Griffin run on fourth and goal from the 2-yard line. Carolina's gap integrity and pursuit nullified Griffin's great speed to the corner, and the Panthers would end up driving the ball 98 yards (thanks to several personal fouls and interference penalties) for a touchdown of their own.

The most active and impressive rookie on the field may have been Carolina rookie linebacker Luke Kuechly out of Boston College, who was credited with 9 tackles and 6 assists on the game. Kuechly is an undersized, active, block-shedding dynamo who is reminiscent of a more athletic version of former Dolphin great Zach Thomas.

A two-play stretch in the fourth quarter illustrated both Washington's lack of offensive rhythm and Carolina's defensive discipline. On successive dropbacks, Griffin was sacked by both Andre Neblett and the emerging Greg Hardy, who came on a twist through the middle of the pocket and sacked Griffin while his eyes were downfield.

After the Redskins loss, head coach Mike Shanahan nearly lost his team for good, saying, "Now you're playing to see who, obviously, is going to be on your football team for years to come. Now we get a chance to evaluate players and see where we're at. Obviously we're not out of it statistically, but now we find out what type of character we've got and how guys keep on fighting through the rest of the season."[17]

It's the kind of comment coaches make after their teams are eliminated from playoff contention. I don't think Shanahan was giving up on the season; rather, I think it was a rare moment of honesty from people (coaches and players) who are usually well-versed in talking without saying anything meaningful. His players weren't pleased.

Shanahan clarified the comment on Monday (somewhat lamely) in a phone interview with ESPN, but the damage had been done. Could the Redskins recover after the bye-week and win any of their remaining five division games? Would Robert Griffin III hit the rookie wall?

"You have a lot of guys that want to win now, people toward the end of their careers who have been here a long time, haven't been to the playoffs in a long time," defensive end Lorenzo Alexander told the *Washington Post*. "Bein' 3-6 really [stinks] because right now we're on the outside looking in. . . . I'm not thinkin' about next year. That's an offseason thing for me. But you know it's hard when you see yourself in that type of position and your head coach is saying those types of things. It's disappointing."[18]

10

GOD AND QUARTERBACKING: FAITH, PROSPERITY, AND PRO FOOTBALL

There's a couple things you don't talk about in life, and that's race, religion and politics," Griffin told a Yahoo! News interviewer when asked about his voting issues. "I try to make sure I don't talk about politics at all."[1]

The political answer is sensible, given that Griffin is charged with not only throwing touchdown passes but also with representing a franchise, selling season ticket licenses, selling shoes, selling sandwiches, and selling jerseys to both Democrats and Republicans alike. Needless to say, that's a lot of pressure. But later in the piece he's equally coy and ambiguous about his faith when asked about how his faith shapes the way he views politics, saying, "It shapes everybody's view. To me, you don't directly relate it, but my faith makes me who I am. When it comes to that, my beliefs are not strict to only what the Bible says. I'm influenced by . . . You probably can't point out exactly what it shapes, but it does shape you."[2]

In a way, Griffin is a refreshing change from the nonstop evangelism of the Tebow brand. It's strange to think that we're already close to entering a post-Tebow NFL, but Tebow's drift out of the spotlight provides an opportunity for a player like Griffin to shine, on and off the field. Griffin certainly seems lower-key about his faith, at least publicly. It's an approach that makes him less polarizing. Griffin's approach will almost certainly change with age as well. By the end of Kurt Warner's amazing run as an NFL quarterback, for example, he was a mature, seasoned public witness.

Griffin is living and playing under a great deal of public pressure. He's the on-field CEO of the most visible corporation in the most political city in the Free World—a city where the word *evangelical* carries some pretty heavy connotations. He's also very young. Still, Griffin has proven that he's unafraid of publicly acknowledging his faith and even talking about it in some depth. He told Black Christian News, "I was heavily influenced by my parents to learn discipline. But my relationship with God was my most important influence. . . . I've been in the church since I was 7. My parents didn't push it on us but they made sure we grew up in the church, so that's all we know, that's what we do." He continued, "Whenever you can be a Christian and come to a Christian university like Baylor and make a difference like this whole football team has, it's great. [God] gives you the stage to make a difference and not to just talk about yourself, but lift Him up. There are a lot of different types of Christians everywhere, but my biggest thing is it's not our job to judge; it's just our job to go out, praise Him, let people know what He's doing, and let people follow if they want to. So I praise God, I thank Him for everything. Purposefully, you live every day for Him, and when He gives you the opportunity to speak up for Him or to do something in His name, you do it."[3]

God certainly seems to be giving Griffin a platform, and, interestingly, like many other kids in their early twenties, he also Tweets religiously (pun intended) and, well, sometimes *religiously* (no pun intended). And his Tweets give us a window into Griffin's theological perspective.

After a home victory over the Baltimore Ravens that may well have saved Washington's season, and in which Griffin sprained his knee, he Tweeted: "Your positive vibes and prayers worked people!!!! To God be the glory!"[4]

What Griffin meant was that tests on his knee came back negative, revealing no tearing in the anterior cruciate ligament that, if present, would have shelved Griffin for the remainder of the season and put a serious damper on Washington's playoff hopes. The Tweet could easily just be construed as more good-vibes positivity from a kid who has consistently emanated them (good vibes) and doesn't necessarily understand all the theological implications of what he's saying (or Tweeting, as it were).

"I think the same pitfalls and dangers plague all young people, whether or not they have faith. And the root problems are consistently narcissism, ignorance and lack of self-control," said Dr. James Spiegel, author of *The Making of an Atheist*, when I asked him about Griffin. "It takes quality parenting [or guardianship of some kind] to train a young person to handle these challenges—to make them self-aware [circumspect] without being self-indulgent. Interestingly, athletics tends to accentuate a kid's movement in either direction, making them more or less morally strong [such that you have remarkable maturity at a young age—e.g, Peyton Manning, Andrew Luck, etc.] or uncommon immaturity and self-indulgence [too many to count]."[5]

For the time being, Griffin seems to be ably navigating the tension between maturity and self-indulgence, even though he probably has every opportunity for self-indulgence waved in front of him each day. Perhaps Griffin's strong connection to his family is helping keep him grounded in the face of temptation.

When asked about his parents' influence at the NFL Combine, he told the media throng, "Military kid, both my parents were in the military. Mom did 12 years, Dad did 21, served in two wars. Discipline was something that was obviously huge. If you say you're going to do something, you do it. If you start it, you finish it. Yes, sir; no, ma'am. You've got to have that kind of structure in your life. It kind of helped me be that disciplined person I am, whether it's with workouts, film, or just the game of football."[6]

Other interesting notes regarding Griffin and faith: He makes the sign of the cross nearly every time Washington takes the field, though he isn't Catholic. Again, I don't know this definitively, but I'll bet he does it partly out of sincere religious affection, and partly because it looks really cool to do so. I would probably do the same thing.

In a way, Griffin's public testimony parallels that of Baylor University, his alma mater, which has itself followed a faith arc like that of many of America's great universities in that it was once grounded on conservative biblical principles and has since drifted in a more culturally compatible direction. Founded in 1841, Baylor's first presidents and administrators were Baptist pastors and missionaries. At one point, Baylor segregated male and female students. During this period the university thrived, as many leaders of the Republic of Texas sent their children there. Eventually, Baylor—settled in Waco, Texas—became racially integrated in 1964, after passage of the Civil Rights Act. Prior to Griffin, Baylor's most famous athletic alum was Hall of Fame linebacker Mike Singletary, who is both African American and an outspoken evangelical Christian.

A shake-up in the Southern Baptist Convention, in which theological conservatives gained an upper hand in the organization, caused the university to adopt a governance less dependent on the Baptist General Convention of Texas, amid fear that they would align with the newly conservative Southern Baptist Convention. As a result it's unclear as to how closely Baylor theologically identifies with its Baptist roots. Probably depends on the individual.

When Griffin was at Baylor, he attended University Baptist Church, which is perhaps better known as the David Crowder Band's church from which Crowder has since moved on. UBC isn't in the charismatic and pentecostal tradition (the kinds of churches in which Griffin grew up), but is probably more hipster/postmodern in its approach. Crowder cofounded the church in 1995 as a response to a need for "relevant" outreach to the Baylor campus. UBC's tagline is "Love God. Embrace Beauty. Live Life to the Fullest"; and its website touts an approach that is "creative without being heretical."[7] Like Baylor, there seems to be both a move to put distance between the church's hipster ethos and its Baptist roots, but also, ultimately, an acceptance of propositional truths communicated in the Nicene Creed on the church's site:

We believe in one Lord, Jesus Christ, the only Son of God, eternally begotten of the Father, God from God, light from light, true God from true God, begotten, not made, of one Being with the Father; through him all things were made. For us and for our salvation he came down from heaven, was incarnate of the Holy Spirit and the Virgin Mary and became truly human. For our sake he was crucified under Pontius Pilate; he suffered death and was buried. On the third day he rose again in accordance with the Scriptures; he ascended into heaven and is seated at the right hand of the Father. He will come again in glory to judge the living and the dead, and his kingdom will have no end.

We believe in the Holy Spirit, the Lord, the giver of life, who proceeds from the Father, who with the Father and the Son is worshiped and glorified, who has spoken through the prophets. We believe in one holy catholic and apostolic Church. We acknowledge one baptism for the forgiveness of sins. We look for the resurrection of the dead, and the life of the world to come.[8]

Interestingly, the UBC website addresses the sacred/secular divide in its "Core Values" section, explaining, "The sacred is said to be more spiritual. Even where a necessary involvement in everyday tasks is acknowledged to be a Christian duty, the work, it is said, has to be done only physically. The spirit within has to be involved in silent communion with God, practicing his presence. The necessity of involvement in the world of people and things is accepted, but the action must be done with the spirit withdrawn into the secret place of union with God, where the 'real' business of life is said to be carried on."[9] This distinction may be what is most difficult and confusing for sports fans who wonder about the role of religion on the field. Pro football seems to mash together the sacred and secular in a way that isn't always clear or helpful.

Either way, though, Griffin, it seems, sought out solid spiritual formation while at Baylor.

"It has been a blast to watch," Crowder told an interviewer from Beliefnet. "It's an unusual feeling around Waco, Texas. We've had a great time with it, watching him on national television has been a riot. Robert has carried himself so well. He's a good dude."[10]

Griffin's faith, it seems, is also driving his boundless confidence and fearless approach to the game. "I don't think about it," he told a *GQ* interviewer when asked about injury. "I know God's gonna protect me and have his angels watching over me no matter what I do. But one thing I've never done, and don't plan on starting to do, is play scared. If you're afraid to get a concussion, you're probably gonna get a concussion."[11]

In the NFL, the line between foxhole theology and just young-guy exuberance and bravado is a very thin one. I say this because Griffin *did* get a concussion, though I'm convinced that the concussion isn't a reflection of his faith, his bravery, or God's faithfulness. It's more just a reflection of the fact that in football, people get concussions.

After a nail-biter of a 17-16 victory over the New York Giants on *Monday Night Football*, Griffin said, "God's on our side. There are a lot more goals this team is striving for. I know we can definitely accomplish them."[12]

Quotes like this either make evangelicals very excited, or scare them to death. In a way these comments can, and should, do both. Griffin gets a mulligan for such comments, largely because they're delivered in the heat of the moment, with a large degree of good-natured exuberance. Is God really on the Redskins' side? It's hard to say. It's also hard to argue with at this point, given the evidence in front of us. Still, there are Christians in every NFL locker room, praying every bit as fervently, who are experiencing the highest of highs and lowest of lows in NFL life. Each week there are Christians leading their teams to victory, and each week there are Christians being benched or released. The Redskins' locker room is no different, as Griffin's backfield mate and fellow Christian Roy Helu Jr. has struggled with lower leg injuries and turf toe this season.

> It's about playing every down like it means everything. It means playing with all of my ability and a total release of all of my talents that God has given me. I want to give the same effort on the first play when my body is fresh and wants to get more yards as I do on the 64th play when I'm dragging my feet and my body is telling me that I can't run over a tackler. I pray throughout the game for strength and focus so I can carry out my assignments. Jesus was focused on His mission when He came down and

walked amongst us. People spit in His face. He could have brought angels down. But He was so focused on doing God's will. I try to take on that mentality, but it only comes through knowing God.[13]

Even though their seasons have been different, Helu and Griffin seem to share their faith in common. However, footage of Griffin giving his testimony at churches, or even extended Griffin interviews on faith, are in short supply.

Robert Griffin III is on television every day, therefore people want to see and read more about Robert Griffin III. There's demand for his product right now, as evidenced by the fact that according to an NFL.com report, Griffin "already has sold more jerseys this year than any player in a single season since the league started tracking the numbers six years ago." The piece goes on to explain that "there is a healthy debate over his NFL Rookie of the Year candidacy with Indianapolis Colts quarterback Andrew Luck, but there's no doubt who resonates most with the public. Luck is sixth in jersey sales."[14]

Winner of Super Bowls I and II, Green Bay's Bart Starr played in a vastly different era as it pertains to the media (the '50s and '60s), but he was far less demonstrative about his faith than Tebow. In general, Starr let his lifestyle and conduct do the talking (as it were) regarding faith, whereas Tebow lets his talking do the talking. Still, Starr didn't downplay or minimize his faith.

And there was a time in the 1990s when it seemed that all former Rams, Giants, and Cardinals quarterback Kurt Warner could talk about was Jesus. Warner wore his faith on his sleeve, had an inspirational once-in-a-lifetime kind of story, and for the most part was embraced by fans both Christian and non-Christian alike. He was outspoken about his faith, but there was a humility about Warner that people connected with, and to his credit he has parlayed that connectivity into a fine post-football television career.

The most public expressions of Christianity in the NFL this season are coming from Baltimore linebacker Ray Lewis, who has announced that he will retire at the end of the season. Lewis, a polarizing figure, seems to be a jumble of contradictions. On one hand, he speaks of God and His plan. On the other, he appears to have evaded a double-murder conviction as one who has barely escaped through the flames. Lewis's bombastic and camera-loving approach to Christianity seems off-putting to some fans. "God is calling," Lewis explained when he announced his retirement. "God is calling in so many other areas of life. . . . He calls me to be a father. 'It's OK to be Daddy.' . . . When I go out, I will make sure that I give Him all the glory."[15]

RG3's secret, at least so far, could be his ability to be all things to all people. White people like him; black people like him; Christians and atheists seem to like him. He seems to be taking a cue from other highly marketable athletes like Michael Jordan and Derek Jeter, neither of whom have ever "done" politics or religion (at least publicly). Griffin is "doing" more religion than Jordan, in that he's a positive-talking athlete from the South who isn't afraid to thank God on occasion, but thus far he hasn't done more than the usual "God helped me overcome adversity" thing. When he was interviewed by NBC Washington upon his arrival, he explained that "you try not to fear too many things. I fear God."[16]

11

COMPARING THE QUARTERBACK CLASSES: 1983, 2004, AND 2012

I'd like to write that I've fished with NFL Hall of Famer Jim Kelly, but that wouldn't exactly be true. I visited Kelly's hunting lodge on the outskirts of Buffalo once—more of a wooden mansion than a lodge, really. It's a place where every square inch of wall is covered with something that Kelly had either killed or pulled out of a lake with his bare hands, where pure testosterone comes out of the taps instead of water. It's a place where Jim Kelly learned that his coauthor (me) couldn't fish. Kelly, then barely fifty years old, moved around the lodge like a much older man—the result of a career full of sacks, concussions, fractured ribs, and separated shoulders bounced off the hard AstroTurf on cold winter afternoons at Rich Stadium in Buffalo. Kelly's days consisted of long soaks in a hot tub and lots of hunting and fishing. Being the showpiece in the legendary 1983 quarterback class didn't come without a price.

As if we needed more proof of the media-saturated jump-the-gun culture we live in, the rookie quarterback class of 2012 is already being compared to the legendary class of 1983 (Elway, Kelly, Marino—all Hall of Famers) and the slightly less legendary class of 2004, which has two multiple Super Bowl champions in Eli Manning and Ben Roethlisberger, and one inconsistent statistical beast in Philip Rivers. To be sure, at least three of 2012's quarterbacks are off to certifiably hot starts—Griffin, Luck, and Seattle's Russell Wilson. But how do their rookie years compare to the rookie years of the quarterbacks mentioned above?

1983

I was seven years old in 1983, but I still remember the dominance wrought by these three quarterbacks, and I still remember what a beast-laden draft 1983 was at *all* positions—not just quarterback. The '83 draft produced Hall of Famers like Eric Dickerson, Bruce (uncle of Clay) Matthews, and Darrell Green, and consistent studs like Jimbo Covert, Chris Hinton, Jim Jeffcoat, and Joey Browner. Interestingly, after the first round in which five were taken, there wasn't another quarterback selected until the fifth round.

John Elway had a relatively dreadful rookie year, going 4-6 in 10 starts, only hitting on 47.5 percent of his passes, and throwing 7 TDs to 14 picks. Elway turned the ball over a lot, throwing 226 career INTs, and didn't truly blossom statistically until he was in his thirties. It's easy to forget that there was a long learning curve for Elway.

By contrast, Kelly's "real" (post-USFL) rookie year was 1986, when he hit almost 60 percent of his passes and threw 22 TDs and only 17 interceptions. He had the benefit of doing postgraduate work in a PlayStation run-and-shoot offense in the USFL and was already an extremely polished passer by the time he arrived as a savior in Buffalo.

Marino had perhaps the most immediately impactful rookie year of the '83 class, throwing 20 TDs and only 6 picks, and leading his team to a 7-2 record in his 9 starts. Statistically, over the course of his career, he was the most impressive of the three, although that could be more a product of Miami's rarely running the ball with any consistency during his tenure.

Todd Blackledge, Kansas City's first rounder, didn't start a game—while New England's Tony Eason only started 4, and the Jets' Kenny O'Brien was an unremarkable 1-4 in his 5 starts. It would have been easy to attach the "bust" label to O'Brien, Elway, or Eason after their rookie years, but it would have been wrong in all cases. O'Brien played in two Pro Bowls, Elway was of course Elway, and even Eason played in a Super Bowl after the 1985 season. The NFL was different in 1983 in that quarterbacks came out of college less prepared to start immediately, and teams generally took more time to develop their starters. Still, it begs the "jumping the gun" question regarding the 2012 class. Are we judging (good or bad) too quickly on these guys? Could Brandon Weeden (who has struggled—or at least is perceived to have struggled) become the next Elway?

2004

The year 2004 was a much more bust-heavy first round than 1983, with names like J. P. Losman, who was yet another Buffalo QB bust, Michael Clayton (Tampa, wide receiver), Kenechi Udeze (health problems, Minnesota), Ahmad Carroll (now playing in Canada), Chris Perry (injuries, Cincy), Rashaun Woods, and Roy Williams—who popularized the inappropriate celebration after a 4-yard catch—topping the list. In 2004, there were many players who just never made an impact at the pro level. Pro Bowl QB Matt Schaub came out of the third round.

Number one overall pick Eli Manning had a pretty dreadful first year, going 1-6 in his starts, hitting on only 47 percent of his passes, and throwing 6 TDs and 9 picks. In was an Elway-esque first year that didn't portend the success that would come for Eli, who has never been a monster stat guy but has had big-game success, including a couple of Super Bowl victories. It's hard to believe that he has more Super Bowl victories than his brother.

Manning's first-round San Diego trade partner, Philip Rivers, sat behind Drew Brees for two seasons, and has since played in four Pro Bowls but has found big-game success elusive. The Chargers always have "great potential" but always seem to find a way to come apart late in the season. Of the three QBs in this class, Rivers is the trickiest to pigeonhole. Statistically he's been as good or better than Manning or Roethlisberger, but has been less consistently reliable than, say, Dan Marino, who was also a statistical beast who didn't win a Super Bowl. Unless something drastic changes, I can't see Rivers winning a Super Bowl or being in the Hall of Fame when it's all said and done. And for what it's worth, he's been the most interpersonally annoying (see: highly publicized trash talk feuds with Peyton Manning and Jay Cutler).

The standout rookie season in 2004 definitely belonged to Big Ben Roethlisberger, who was a perfect 13-0 in his starts, hit on 66 percent of a his passes, and threw 17 TDs and 11 picks, snagging the AP Offensive Rookie of the Year honor in the process. It could be argued that Ben went to the best franchise of the three, as Pittsburgh has always been the picture of stability and was the most talent-laden and ready to win. Roethlisberger's career has largely been an extension of the kind of moxie and consistency he showed as a rookie.

2012

This year's draft featured five quarterbacks selected in the first round, whom I'll break down statistically.

Andrew Luck is an astonishing 11-5 in his regular season starts—astonishing because the Colts were so awful last year, looking lost without Peyton Manning and going 2-14 in the process. Luck has been aided by T. Y. Hilton, who is fast becoming a sensation at wide receiver; two rookie TE talents in Dwayne Allen and Luck's college teammate, Coby Fleener; and the steady veteran Reggie Wayne, who still has fuel in the proverbial tank. Luck hit 54 percent of his passes with 23 TDs and 18 INTs. Luck can make plays with his feet, and generally makes smart decisions with the football while still knowing how and when to take a shot. And he's doing it all without the luxury of a running game, which Indy hasn't had in years (since Edgerrin James left). By comparison, Peyton Manning hit 56 percent of his passes as a rookie and threw 26 touchdowns and 28 picks while struggling to a 3-13 record.

Statistically, Robert Griffin III has been even more impressive, albeit in a completely different offensive scheme with completely different responsibilities. Relying heavily on a beastly running game (to which he's a key contributor), many of Griffin's downfield throws come off play-action, but he's still been razor sharp, hitting 66 percent of his throws with 20 touchdowns compared to only 5 picks. He keeps the 'Skins competitive in every game they're playing, leading them to a 9-6 record in his starts and keeping a once moribund franchise in playoff contention.

Ryan Tannehill has gone 7-9 in his starts and has struggled with turning the ball over, throwing only 12 TDs and 13 picks, though as I've mentioned before, he probably has the worst supporting cast of the group. Interestingly, Brandon Weeden of Cleveland is perceived as

131

having a worse season than any of the other first-rounders, yet he's completing passes at nearly the same clip (57 percent) as Tannehill, has a slightly worse record (5-10), and has thrown more touchdowns (14) than his counterpart in Miami. Perhaps it has something to do with his age, or the pessimism of the media, or the perceived "upside" of the young and athletic Tannehill, but the numbers show that Weeden is probably having a better season. For what it's worth, they're both having better seasons (at least statistically, and in the win-loss column) than Hall of Famer Troy Aikman did in his rookie year in Dallas.

The X factor in this year's class is Russell Wilson, who would be the story of the year in any year that didn't also contain Andrew Luck and RG3. Wilson has been a beast for Seattle. He's thrown 26 TDs, only 10 picks, and is hitting over 60 percent of his passes. More importantly, he led Seattle to a 10-5 record in his starts and has engineered game winning drives over Green Bay, New England, and Chicago. Not bad. He looks to be the steal of the draft thus far and would be a national sensation were he not playing in an obscure media market.

The question, not only for this year's Rookie of the Year race but for the future, is which elite quarterback—Luck or Griffin (or, to be fair, Wilson)—will be a better long-term answer for his respective team? Luck and the Colts both seem to be far exceeding expectations this year, as 2011's Colts squad was one of the worst NFL teams, on a week-to-week basis, in recent memory. The Colts made definitive changes to their roster, mainly through the draft, and rookies like tight end Coby Fleener and wide receiver T. Y. Hilton are making huge impacts. And clearly, with head coach Chuck Pagano battling cancer and Bruce Arians filling in admirably, they're playing for the elusive "something more."

Wilson may benefit from playing with the most complete offensive unit at this stage. He has a backfield workhorse in Marshawn Lynch, who is in the prime of his career, and has a solid, veteran offensive line in front of him. Wilson doesn't have one dominant go-to receiver, but he spreads the ball to a variety of talented wideouts and tight ends.

For his part, Griffin is operating in an offense that, like Luck's, has lots of young, talented skill players with upside as well. It's safe to assume that Alfred Morris, Leonard Hankerson, Fred Davis, and Washington's other skill players will continue to develop alongside their quarterback. Griffin's offense also seems uniquely tailored to maximize his unique skill set; and given Mike Shanahan's track record for quarterback development, it's safe to assume that he'll begin to limit the risks he takes with RG3's body with an eye toward the future.

12

PURSUIT OF PERFECTION

Part of what's easy to love about Robert Griffin is his own perception of invincibility. It's a compelling thing to watch someone who thinks he's unstoppable and unbreakable. Jordan was that way. Bo Jackson was that way before his injury. They were athletically blessed people operating at a higher level than their already elite peers. In a two-week stretch in November, the Eagle and Cowboy games represented the best of Robert Griffin and the Washington Redskins, and fueled their unlikely assault on the top of the NFC East.

A bye-week seemed to heal the wounds that came after Shanahan's unfortunate postgame comments—comments that were clarified and put into perspective before the team left for the bye.

"I think the same leniency that you want to give players after the game—Coach was upset, get his thoughts together—I think should be applied in this situation as far as Coach Shanahan is concerned," Kedric Golston explained to the *Washington Post*. "This is the NFL. We're always being evaluated, you know what I mean. You want guys that want to play. It's easy to play when you're winning and everything's good. But you find out the true character of a man when things are down. Tough times don't last. Tough people do. So the fact of the matter is, it's not what Coach Shanahan said. It's about how we respond coming out of this bye when we play Philly."[1]

Philly is in the midst of its own 5-game losing streak and, sitting at an identical 3-6, seems to be playing to salvage coach Andy Reid's job. While this long-standing NFC East rivalry usually offers fireworks and ill tempers, the excitement of the game is lessened somewhat by the fact that the Eagles' starting quarterback, Mike Vick, is sidelined with a concussion. According to reports, Vick's symptoms even a week later include nausea, sensitivity to light, sleeping all day, and a lack of balance. He didn't even make the trip with the Eagles.

Into his place steps rookie quarterback Nick Foles—a third-round draft choice from Arizona, where he threw 67 touchdown passes—charged with breathing life into Philadelphia's anemic (17 points per game) offense. Surprisingly, Washington is in the midst of an 8-game losing streak against rookie quarterbacks.

The Redskins are staring down a 3-game stretch against Philly, Dallas, and the New York Giants (all divisional opponents) that will determine the fate of their season. Even at 3-6, the playoffs are still a mathematical possibility, and this game has the feel of a playoff. The loser, truly, is done.

Nick Foles gets the ball in his hands first, working behind a patchwork offensive line that is on its fifth lineup change of the season. Foles has the look of a classic NFL quarterback—big-bodied and tall in the pocket, but relatively immobile. His first series ends on an interception that isn't his fault, as a strike to tight end Brent Celek bounces off Celek's chest and right into the waiting arms of DeAngelo Hall, who returns it 22 yards.

A few plays later Griffin's first pass comes out of the pistol formation (short shotgun) and is a play-action strike to fullback Darrel Young for 9 yards and a touchdown.

Philly experiments with short, three-step drops and eight-man protection schemes to keep Foles upright, but frankly they already have the look of a beaten, demoralized team that is playing out the proverbial string. Foles's second drive ends on an ill-advised floater, snatched away by Redskins safety Brandon Merriweather, who is seeing his first game action since a bizarre pregame warm-up injury early in the season.

The Redskins essentially salt the game away in the second quarter on a double play-action fake in which Griffin fakes a stretch to Alfred Morris, fakes an end-around to Brandon Banks, and then lofts a 49-yard strike to the ridiculously wide-open Aldrick Robinson over the top of the overpaid Nnamdi Asomugha, whose tenure in Philadelphia has been nothing short of disastrous. Asomugha was a part of what was supposed to be an "All-Star" defense, which has been anything but. Asomugha was playing Robinson way to the outside, as though he expected help from the middle, which never came.

Griffin flat-out gets lucky in the third quarter, throwing a ball that showcases his arm talent (traveling 65 yards in the air) right into double coverage. Somehow Santana Moss goes up between two defenders, snatches the ball out of the air, and breaks a tackle to fall into the end zone. In the books it's a 61-yard touchdown pass, but it should have been an interception and is instead the de facto end of the 2012 Philadelphia Eagles. Griffin would only attempt two more passes the rest of the afternoon, one of which was a 22-yard seam route to tight end Logan Paulsen, who was an undrafted free agent in 2010.

"Nothing's going to change; Robert's going to go out there and be special," Santana Moss told reporters after the game. "That's the gift that he has, he's a special guy. He brings that kind of 'specialness.' I don't know if that's a word, but he brings it to our offense."[2]

Griffin finished 14 of 15 for an even 200 yards passing, adding another 84 yards on the ground in a nearly flawless performance that suddenly breathed new life into the Redskins faithful. He was serenaded with chants of "RG! RG!" as he left the field with only a few days before a Thanksgiving showdown in Dallas.

———

While Thursday games are a ratings boon, they can be nightmarish for NFL players, whose recovery and preparation process starts immediately after the end of their Sunday games. Players are fast-tracked through training rooms to assess and treat injuries, and have only two real practice days to prepare for their Thursday opponents. Add to that film study, travel, and time it takes to recover from the previous game's soreness . . . and players face a tall order on Thursday.

Both Thanksgiving Day fixtures, Washington faces the Cowboys—who are 6-0 all-time against Washington and have won 22 of the last 29 overall in the series. Coming into the game an even 5-5, the Cowboys have their sights set on the top of a parity-laden NFC East in which nobody is looking horrible, but nobody's actually looking good either. Dallas's exciting but inconsistent quarterback, Tony Romo, appears to be settling down as well. Romo tossed up 13 interceptions through Week 7, but hasn't thrown one in the last 3 games.

"[The Redskins] are certainly playing different offensive football than they've played in the past because of RGIII being their quarterback," head coach Jason Garrett told the Cowboys' official website. "We certainly have to do our best to get on top of what they're trying to get done. They've certainly been very impressive at different times and they do a variety of things, and we've got to make sure we can contain him."[3]

Coaches can sometimes be masters of stating the obvious. And contain him they would, largely, with Dallas holding Griffin to just 29 yards. But fellow rookie Alfred Morris would top 100 yards again (113), and what Griffin would do was pass. Specifically, for 4 touchdowns, for the second week in a row. But his first series started slowly, with Griffin falling down after handing the ball to Alfred Morris on the first play and then taking an intentional grounding call on third down. However, the offense would never really look back.

In the second quarter, Griffin lined up with wide receiver Aldrick Robinson flanked to the right of the formation. Robinson, a sixth-round draft choice and a local product from Southern Methodist University, possesses legit 4.42 40-yard-dash speed, but found his stock falling because of questions about his hands. As usual, Griffin froze free safety Danny McCray with a run fake, and McCray's split-second hesitation allowed Robinson to blaze by the big safety (6 feet 1 inch, 222 pounds) from LSU.

"I've never seen the primary receiver open as often as the Redskins get their primary receiver open," explained ESPN's Trent Dilfer in a radio interview with *The Sports Fix* on ESPN 980 December 6, 2012. "It's quite simply the best first- and second-down offense I've ever seen." Dilfer explained that Washington's primary formation, the "pistol [short shotgun]," was pioneered by Nevada coach Chris Ault in 2005. The pistol, which aligns an I-back behind the quarterback and two backs on each side of the quarterback, allows the Redskins to run each of the zone-read fakes that Griffin became accustomed to in college, while still allowing for a full complement of play-action fakes and routes.

Still, some critique the sustainability of the offense. "He's a big dude now too," says Dilfer. "He's a beast. He's a thick-jointed country-strong young man. He's gonna hold up fine at ten carries per game. When you don't understand something you tend to criticize it . . . because it doesn't fit your paradigm," says Dilfer of Griffin's new, run-oriented approach to quarterbacking.

"If you put all your chips in on stopping the zone read," Dilfer explains, "you've made yourself vulnerable to traditional runs. I think he's gonna develop into a complete passer. I think he'll develop into what I call a quarterback surgeon . . . the best of the best. They only run a few concepts in their passing game, but they run them over and over and run them perfectly."

"He's handled the enormity of the job as well as anybody can," Dilfer says. "It makes me want to move to the DC area and become a fan. For the next 10–12 years this is going to be a special, special story."[4]

The 'Skins quickly regained possession again after Dallas's troubled but talented playmaker Dez Bryant was stripped by Josh Wilson—a fumble that was recovered by safety DeJon Gomes. The Redskins then embarked on a balanced drive, mixing runs by Morris, a short but clutch pass to Santana Moss in which Griffin squeezed the ball into the smallest of windows, and finally a play-action skinny post to Garçon for 19 in which both Dallas linebackers jumped the run fake so vigorously that there was literally no one on the second level to challenge Garçon.

Griffin's passing has been so effective in part because of Shanahan's commitment to the run game. The Redskins run the ball 51 percent of the time and have the number two rush offense in the entire league. Granted, those numbers are somewhat inflated by the presence of Griffin, but even without him they would still be one of the better rush offenses in the league. It's fitting, then, that an Alfred Morris plunge from the 1-yard line put Washington on top 14-3.

After another Dallas three-and-out, Griffin and the play-action passing game struck again. After a short strike to Brandon Banks, Griffin again faked and then hit Pierre Garçon on a deep crossing route. Garçon had to perform a complete 180-degree turn to catch the ball behind him, then explode upfield, showing both the short-area quickness and the long speed that made him one of the most handsomely paid free agents last offseason. It was an impressive strike by Griffin, but Garçon's explosiveness turned it into a touchdown. It seemed the rout was on in earnest.

"As Pierre is running on his long touchdown, and I was like, 'Man, that was a great catch,'" Griffin told the media after the game. "I had to throw it to only that spot, and you don't see many guys make catches like that."[5]

On Dallas's next drive, Tony Romo made another poor decision, this time throwing late over the middle to Cole Beasley. Redskins cornerback DeAngelo Hall jumped the route and returned the ball to the Dallas 33 with thirty seconds remaining on the clock—an eternity in RG3 time.

Griffin started the drive with a sack. He still seems, at times, a little frozen in the pocket and will with more reps develop the Roethlisberger-esque sense for where and how to move to avoid rushers. In fact, Dallas sacked him 4 times and knocked him down on several other occasions. He then threw short to Joshua Morgan for 11, before Alfred Morris burst up the middle for 16 as several defenders followed a faking Griffin. The play is a great example of offensive philosophy and how certain plays set up other plays. There's the sense that there's order and theory behind everything the Redskins are doing.

After their third time-out, Griffin rolled to his right and threw a sublime back-shoulder strike along the end zone sideline to Santana Moss. To put Moss's production into perspective, he has only 25 catches on the season, but 7 of them are for touchdowns and they all, it seems, came at clutch and opportune times.

Tony Romo would mount a valiant third-quarter comeback attempt—including the longest TD pass of his career, an 85-yarder to Dez Bryant—but Griffin would put the game out of reach with another scoring strike to backup tight end Niles Paul. The final score was 38-31, but it didn't really feel that close. The Redskins hadn't won on Thanksgiving Day since beating Detroit in 1973.

"Anytime you have a guy like him, you never worry about him," said Washington cornerback DeAngelo Hall of Griffin. "You worry about the guys around him being able to keep up with the pace."

Mike Shanahan's assessment of his quarterback, postgame, was more direct. "He's kind of like 'Cool Hand Luke,'" Shanahan said. "He doesn't get too upset about anything."[6]

13

VICK, IRONY, AND INJURY

As the Washington Redskins rehabilitate Robert Griffin's knee in anticipation of their Week 16 matchup with Philadelphia, demoted Eagles quarterback Michael Vick, now third string, is running the Eagles scout team pretending to be Robert Griffin III. As a "scout team" quarterback, your job is to emulate the other team's quarterback in practice.

Vick, when asked what it was like to emulate the rookie, recognizes that RG3 is a much younger player. Showing uncanny maturity and perspective, he says, "I can't be upset or disgruntled about anything that happens, it's just a blessing to be back playing football, from where I came from, and the opportunities that I've had over the last 3 or 4 years, I would have never thought. This is what I love, and I realized that today, out there throwing balls on the scout team."[1]

There's a gospel sweetness in Vick's story, and the image of a humbled but joyful former star throwing passes in a scout team jersey actually makes me smile for Vick. It's a uniquely humbling thing to have your sins and flaws laid bare before the world, to pay your penalty, to receive

Christ's pardon, and then to have a chance to joyfully pursue your life anew. It's a thrill to be able to see Vick living his life again. There is talk of him leaving Philly in the Andy Reid purge and hooking on somewhere else as a starter, and although he appears to have entered the Aaron Brooks/Jeff Blake/Daunte Culpepper twilight of his career, he seems to be handling it with class.

In his own locker room, Griffin was greeted by a $10,000 fine from league offices for wearing an Adidas sweat suit (Griffin's exclusive apparel sponsor) to a postgame press conference in a league that has an exclusive uniform contract with Nike. Such is life in the modern NFL. These are, as some say, "first-world" problems. The only drama comes in wondering if Adidas will pick up the fine.

———

After an unlikely and sensational 3-game divisional win-streak against Philadelphia, Dallas, and the New York Giants on *Monday Night Football*, Griffin and the Redskins pulled out a come-from-behind-overtime showstopper against Baltimore.

The Ravens came into the game as defensively toothless as they've been in years, surrendering 125.8 yards per game on the ground and 372.3 total yards—both the most in team history. Against Washington they'd be going without linebackers Dannell Ellerbe, Ray Lewis, and Terrell Suggs. Meanwhile, Washington came into the game leading the league in rushing and on pace to set a franchise record in rushing yards in a season. Fitting, then, that on the first play Alfred Morris gashed Baltimore for 29, and on the second play exploded again on another 21-yard run that was called back due to a holding penalty. But it was too late for Baltimore—blood had been drawn and the damage was done. The opening drive ended on a 4-yard pass to Joshua Morgan on a play in which Griffin deftly avoided the rush and kept the play alive with his feet.

Relatively speaking, Griffin was held in check before his injury, going 15-26 for 246 yards and a score. More importantly, he didn't turn the ball over, and the threat of Griffin as a runner and a passer opened things up for Morris, who had 122 rushing yards and a touchdown against a team that used to be a brick wall for opposing runners.

The Redskins trailed 28-20 in the fourth quarter after a touchdown by Baltimore running back Ray Rice. After the Redskins took possession (and kept it on a controversial, and long, replay on the kickoff), Griffin began to move the team, mixing short passes to Santana Moss and Leonard Hankerson. After taking a sack by Paul Kruger, Griffin was on the run again on the next play, which in many ways just looked like a standard Griffin scramble. But as he was going down, his right leg whipped into Ravens defensive tackle Haloti Ngata. Griffin knew immediately that something was amiss.

"I knew as soon as I got hit," he said afterward. "I screamed. Like a man, of course. It hurt really bad."[2]

Griffin left for a play and then returned for four more, hopping valiantly on one leg and getting the Redskins into Ravens territory. Finally he dropped to all fours and was helped of the field by the Redskins training staff. "I knew I needed to get out at that point," he said. "At some point you have to do what's right for the team."[3]

What was right for the team was for backup quarterback Kirk Cousins, the most decorated passer in Michigan State University history, to get his opportunity. The rest, as they say, is history. Cousins, who had only played sparingly in the Atlanta game, came off the bench to engineer a game-winning drive culminating in an 11-yard scoring strike to Pierre Garçon. He then did his best to channel RG3, running in the 2-point conversion to send the game into overtime.

"It was awesome," said Griffin of the Cousins series.[4]

"He's ice," said wide receiver Joshua Morgan. "Like they used to say about Larry Bird, he got ice water in his veins. That's the best thing you can say about Kirk. He was coming like nothing was even going on."[5]

Another rookie, Richard Crawford, returned a punt 64 yards in overtime to set up Kai Forbath's game-winning field goal and sealing Washington's fourth win in as many games. As for Griffin's injury and his availability for the end of the season and a potential playoff run, time would tell. He was limping in a large brace after the game.

"I'm not a doctor, but I know what an ACL feels like," he said. "And it doesn't feel like an ACL. . . . If I felt that, I'd be pretty nervous. But we won the game, everybody's praying for me, I feel pretty good right now about the whole situation. I'm not too nervous, but I'll definitely be praying during the MRI."[6]

———

Griffin's MRI came out clear, but he wouldn't get to start the following weekend at Cleveland—that job would again go to Cousins, who looked cool, comfortable, and efficient in his first extended action as a pro, going 26 of 37 for 329 yards, 2 TDs, and a pick. With the exception of the read-option, the offense didn't change much. Cousins ran Alfred Morris liberally (27 attempts) to set up the play-action game that Washington has used all season. According to ESPN Research, Washington has now passed for a league-leading 1,980 yards this season after play-action fakes; and on the game, Cousins was 15-19 on play-action.

Cousins was considered a steal as a fourth-round draft choice, and presented the Redskins with a tantalizing option on Draft Day. Rather than add a player at another position of need, they chose to add a player, in Cousins, that many teams considered a first or second round value and who projected as an NFL starter. His play against Baltimore and Cleveland proved that the Redskins made the right decision.

Cousins went three-and-out on his first series featuring a false start and an incompletion. On his second series, Cousins threw an interception. After four possessions, the Redskins had gained a total of 7 yards. Cousins was 1-for-6 for 4 yards, with the interception.

His interception led to the Browns' first score, but afterward, Cousins relaxed, settled in, and played a nearly perfect game, throwing 2 touchdown strikes to Leonard Hankerson. His biggest fan may have been Griffin, who was a Fox Television fixture on the sidelines, shown adjusting his hat, listening to booth chatter on the headphones, bonding with Rex Grossman, hugging Mike Shanahan, and generally cultivating the "supportive, carefree good guy" image he has cultivated thus far.

Across the field, Browns rookies Brandon Weeden and Trent Richardson struggled mightily. Weeden threw 2 interceptions, and Richardson managed only 28 yards.

Washington's Week 16 matchup in Philadelphia features two teams going in different directions. The Redskins control their playoff destiny, while Philadelphia sits at 4-11 and starts rookie quarterback Nick Foles, who has completed 59 percent of his passes for 1,354 yards—second-best for a rookie in team history. There's a rebuilding feel in the air, as it is almost certain that Andy Reid will be gone at the end of the season. The Eagles have already parted ways with high-priced DE Jason Babin (who was quickly picked up by Jacksonville) and are beginning to phase young players like running back Bryce Brown into the lineup.

Foles is looking more comfortable with each start, and today the Eagles control the ball for the first five minutes of the game, going for it twice on fourth down. The first time, Foles half-rolls to his left (nonthrowing side) and hits tight end Brent Celek. At the end of the drive Foles hits receiver Jeremy Maclin in the corner of the end zone for 28 yards and a score. Foles knew he could take a shot as the Redskins jumped offside on the play, and his shot paid off.

Washington's first series starts rough, with Alfred Morris bottled up on successive carries. For the first time all season, the Redskins are without tackle Tyler Polumbus, who is out with a concussion. Griffin is back on the field, however, after resting the previous week in Cleveland, but he's on the field with a large, bulky knee brace and clearly doesn't look like himself. Still, he drops back and fires a laser on third down to Leonard Hankerson to move the chains. Later in the series he goes downfield on a play-action pass to Garçon, dropping the ball behind the linebackers and in front of Philadelphia's safeties who are in two-deep coverage. However, on the next play he limps out of bounds on a designed run, clearly lacking explosiveness. It would be his last designed run of the day.

He misfires into coverage on third and 2, and then has a fourth-down rollout blown up by Eagles defensive end Brandon Graham, who has racked up 4 sacks since Babin's release.

The Redskins score their first touchdown with 3:36 remaining in the first half on a swing pass to Joshua Morgan that acts more like a long handoff. Morgan darts into the end zone behind a sustained block by Pierre Garçon.

Griffin opens the second half sharply, hitting a play-action post-corner route for 29 yards in which Garçon goes up to snatch a high ball. On the next play Griffin goes play-action again, hitting athletic hybrid WR/TE Niles Paul on a rollout for 21 yards. Paul, 6 feet 1 inch and 233 pounds, is an example of the Shanahan propensity for taking projects and molding them into stars. He expects a Shannon Sharpe–like impact out of Paul eventually, as the two share similar physical characteristics.

"Paul is like Shannon Sharpe, but faster," fullback Darrel Young said to Redskins.com in the preseason. "He is the next Shannon Sharpe, and you can quote me on that."[7]

In the preseason, Shanahan invited Sharpe (whom he coached in Denver) to Redskins Park to address the team and the newly converted tight end. Paul, a fifth-round pick, caught 103 passes for 1,532 yards and 5 touchdowns at Nebraska. An incredibly versatile athlete, he was also a Second-Team All-Big 12 punt and kickoff returner.

"Sharpe told me that I'm a smaller guy and I'm not going to win every battle," Paul said. "My role is to protect the running back and the quarterback. As long as I'm doing my job, that's all that matters."[8]

"Niles is a competitor, he's a worker. He has all of it," veteran tight end Chris Cooley said. "He's explosive, he's learning, and he's getting better."[9] Cooley would record his first reception of the season in the fourth quarter, making 428 for his career. He's clearly near the end of his career—usurped by younger, more athletic players like Paul, Logan Paulsen, and the injured Fred Davis—but he will contribute to the team's playoff run.

At the end of the fourth quarter, the Redskins line up in the shotgun on three straight plays and benefit from three great runs of 5, 10, and 6 yards by Morris. Royster then comes off the bench and goes for 7 of his own as Shanahan clearly leans more heavily on his running backs with a hobbled Griffin in the backfield. Forced out of his running ways, Griffin becomes more of a traditional pocket quarterback against Philadelphia, and later in the drive he finds Santana Moss singled up on safety Colt Anderson—a matchup the Redskins want to exploit. Griffin drops the ball perfectly into the back left corner of the end zone, where Moss gathers it in and drags his feet for the score. The score puts the Redskins ahead 27-13 and is an example of Griffin's ball-distribution genius. Unlike Chicago's Jay Cutler, who has set a single-season record for targeting the same receiver (Brandon Marshall), Washington's final (season) receiving stats are a testimony to Griffin's ability to feed different receivers:

PLAYER	REC.	YARDS	YPC	LONG	TD
Josh Morgan	48	510	10.6	32	2
Pierre Garçon	44	633	14.4	88	4
Santana Moss	41	573	14.0	77	8
Leonard Hankerson	38	543	14.3	68	3
Logan Paulsen	25	308	12.3	31	1

Griffin finished the game with pretty pedestrian numbers—only 4 yards rushing, and 16 of 24 passing for 198 yards. Still, he came up with big throws when it mattered, propelling his team one step closer to a playoff appearance.

"Anytime you wear a brace, it's going to restrict your motion," Griffin said after the game. "It didn't slow me down by any means. I felt like myself out there. That's why they call me quarterback. It's not abbreviated with running quarterback. I have to throw the ball and assist guys by handing off."[10]

"He's a guy we count on to lead us," said Moss of Griffin after the game. "He's a born leader and he came in here with that mentality. We are very fortunate to have him."[11] At this point in the season, Griffin's leadership appears to have matured from reaching out and involving his teammates early on, to playing hurt and sacrificing his body for them at this crucial stage. More than leading with his words, Griffin is leading with his health and his future. The question this begs is, of course, how long can he keep it up? And does playing hurt today threaten his ability to lead his team tomorrow?

Griffin has even begun to talk like a veteran, working hard to keep each game in its proper perspective. The Redskins, who had been fighting for their season, would put this win in context and then move on quickly. "We're already onto the next one," Griffin said afterward. "You don't celebrate wins at this point in the season."[12]

EPILOGUE

HE'LL NEVER BE NEW AGAIN

The last week of the regular season brought with it a variety of quarterback-related story lines. Rumor had it that embattled running quarterback Tim Tebow would soon be on his way to Jacksonville in what would be a semidesperate move on the part of owner Shad Khan to sell some jerseys and seat licenses. Chad Henne's dreadful performance at Tennessee wasn't hurting Tebow's chances. If Tebow indeed ends up in Jacksonville, it will be his third team. It will also, undoubtedly, be his last chance at being a real, starting NFL quarterback.

While Henne and Tennessee's Locker struggled, and while Mark Sanchez played out the proverbial string in New York, Tebow sat on the bench. These quarterbacks may both—along with their coaches—be gone next season. Mike Vick, in what may be his last NFL start (only because Nick Foles was hurt), endured a 42-7 drubbing at the hands of the New York Giants; and his coach, Andy Reid, was fired before sundown. On the West Coast, Oakland backup Terrelle Pryor, a poor-man's Cam Newton, made his first NFL start and acquitted himself well, throwing for two scores and running for another. In Minnesota, Adrian Peterson came within 9 yards of Eric Dickersons's single-season rushing record, and Andrew Luck passed the Colts to a win over Houston in head coach Chuck Pagano's emotional return. The Colts, at 11-5, are for real. So is their rookie quarterback.

My midseason quarterback ranking may have been a little premature, as it looks like there are several teams—the Jets, Chiefs, Raiders, Cardinals, Jaguars, Eagles, and Bills among them—who will be shopping for new signal-callers before next season. Coaches who may soon be unemployed include Romeo Crennel, Rex Ryan, Ron Rivera, Norv Turner, Pat Shurmur, Ken Whisenhunt, Chan Gailey, Mike Mularkey (maybe), and Mike Munchak (maybe). It's no accident that bad quarterbacking and coaching struggles often go hand in hand.

———

After 9 games the Redskins were 3-6. They named a rookie, RG3, team captain—almost unheard of in NFL circles. They haven't lost since. Griffin has thrown 20 touchdowns, only 5 picks, and was the first rookie quarterback in NFL history to be unanimously voted to the Pro Bowl. Against Dallas at home, he and the Redskins control their own playoff destiny. Quite simply, if they win they're in.

Griffin goes 3-and-out on the first series in the face of a DeMarcus Ware pass rush. His pass hits Joshua Morgan in the hands and the ball is dropped. It's a problem that (at Pittsburgh specifically) has plagued the Redskins. Later in the first quarter he runs for a first down—around Ware—and takes a shot on his big, bulky knee-brace. The play—a shotgun dive-option—is a staple of Washington's offense. In it, they (illogically, but stay with me) leave Ware unblocked, and if he sucks in on the dive back, Griffin is to pull the ball and run around the end. If he stays put, Griffin gives the ball up to Morris. It's a simple play, but it has befuddled Washington's opponents all season. Still, when Griffin takes a shot, all of Washington holds its collective breath. Later, kicker Kai Forbath's hot streak comes to an untimely end as he misses his first field goal of the season. The game already has a strange feel to it, and it will get stranger.

Dallas quarterback Tony Romo's poorly thrown interceptions are keeping Washington's offense on the field, even though Griffin and the Redskins look as rhythmless and frustrated as they have in a while. Griffin looks like he's trying to force balls into coverage, and his passes appear to lack zip—perhaps as a result of his banged-up knee. "This is not the Robert Griffin III we've seen earlier," says analyst Chris Collinsworth during the network telecast. He's right. He throws a couple of sloppy passes up for grabs and misses an open Santana Moss on a short out route that would have picked up a first down.

Griffin has had at least a half season (probably more) of people saying he's the greatest thing since sliced bread, and he may be in danger of believing the hype. And watching Dallas tight end Jason Witten catch his 800th ball, it occurs to me that we're too quick to anoint these guys. Last year's tight-end-of-the-moment, Jimmy Graham (New Orleans), was going to redefine the position. Two years ago Green Bay tight end Jermichael Finley was going to redefine the position. Both were relatively quiet this season. One of the drawbacks of our digital age is we lose our ability to fully appreciate a veteran like Witten or Tony Gonzales. I think the same could be said of the quarterback position.

Part of the beauty of Tony Romo is that he can throw a pair of horrific interceptions and then forget about them completely, allowing him to drive his team down the field, keep a third down in the red-zone alive forever with his legs, and then throw a floater into the end zone to Jason Witten.

It is only Alfred Morris keeping the Washington offense competitive. He continually runs through tackles. On a run-dominated drive near the end of the second quarter, Griffin limps for a first down but clearly isn't the same. A play later he hands off to Alfred Morris, who gallops into the end zone to tie the score. On a night whose hype is dominated by RG3, it's Morris who's carrying the load. By halftime, Griffin has only 43 yards passing and another 21 on the ground. Later, Morris sets the franchise record for rushing yards in a season, eclipsing the mark held by Clinton Portis.

Drops continue to plague the Redskins. In the third, on a third down and 2, Griffin hobbles into his drop and throws a strike into the chest of Pierre Garçon. The ball falls harmlessly to the turf and the Redskins, again, are forced to punt.

Near the end of the third quarter, Griffin's passing game comes alive. On successive plays he hits the play-action post to Garçon that has been the club's specialty, and then on the next play it's a perfectly executed bubble screen. A play after that Griffin limps, untouched, into the end zone after a deft zone-read fake to Morris. Just like that, Washington is in the driver's seat.

In the fourth, Griffin's heating-up process appears to have come to fruition as, physically, he looks like a new player. On many of the zone-read plays, All-World Cowboy OLB DeMarcus Ware is left unblocked while Griffin runs wild around his corner. Albert Morris's career night continues with a 32-yard touchdown on a toss sweep, in which he appears to weave through the entire Cowboy defense.

It's fitting that linebacker London Fletcher, coming on a blitz, basically ends the game in the fourth quarter—fitting because Fletcher has been such an underrated soldier for so long. On a third and 10, Romo drops back to throw, turns his back, and is corralled by Fletcher. Star receiver Dez Bryant was hurt on the play and is, along with Miles Austin, potentially done for the evening. The game, and Dallas's season, is effectively over. It's a game that almost perfectly encapsulates the Tony Romo regime in Dallas—a regime in which some sensational plays have been followed by some mistakes that have kept Dallas from any kind of consistent success. For what it's worth, each of Romo's interceptions were thrown from his back foot. Mechanics matter.

To put the game into perspective for Washington, Griffin basically played poorly for at least a half, yet he still didn't turn the ball over and still didn't really hurt his team. His greatest strength may be knowing when not to push the ball downfield. The Redskins were able to ride the consistent running of Alfred Morris into the playoffs. By the middle of the fourth quarter, he has 180 yards and is averaging a gaudy 7.2 yards per carry. Only Eric Dickerson and George Rodgers have rushed for more yards as a rookie.

———

One of my favorite scenes in Peter Berg's beautiful 2004 film *Friday Night Lights* (based on Buzz Bissinger's terrific book by the same name) is a scene in which gifted running back James "Boobie" Miles suffers a devastating knee injury; but, in the throes of youthful invincibility and outright denial, he declares himself healthy enough to play later in the season. He rushes to the locker room exuberantly and suits up, then walks out of the tunnel clad in his gear in front of his team's fans and raises a fist defiantly. I love the scene because Miles beautifully represents everything great about being young and feeling invincible.

The Miles story, of course, is tragic. Later in that game he is given an opportunity to carry the ball and reinjures his ravaged knee—falling to the turf without being touched by an opponent. He is never the same again.

My feeling going into Washington's Wild Card game was that they were going into battle with a one-legged quarterback, and that the condition of Griffin's knee—the most talked about joint in Washington DC since Bill Clinton's first presidential campaign—was worse than anyone let on. These fears were confirmed late in the week in *USA Today* by Dr. James Andrews, a seventy-year-old orthopedic surgeon whose relationship with the Washington Redskins isn't exactly clear. Nonetheless, he was on the sidelines for the Baltimore game in which Griffin was injured, and he wasn't entirely convinced of the player's health.

"[Griffin] didn't even let us look at him," Andrews said. "He came off the field, walked through the sidelines, circled back through the players and took off back to the field. It wasn't our opinion.

"We didn't even get to touch him or talk to him. Scared the hell out of me."[1]

Griffin came out of the game, for good, a few plays later, but suited up against the Eagles and the Cowboys, essentially playing on one good leg to end the season. Andrews, it should be noted, is probably the most celebrated orthopedic surgeon in professional sports—having performed the original Tommy John surgery and being known for his work on stars like Tom Brady, Drew Brees, and Marcus Lattimore.

The Andrews quote set off a flurry of media activity and scrutiny, much of it aimed at Mike Shanahan, who was accused of playing fast and loose with the franchise quarterback. Clearly, Griffin shouldn't have gone back into the game against Baltimore, and it could be argued that he shouldn't have played against Philly or Dallas either. It's easy to second-guess from the sidelines—especially in the area of battlefield medicine—but everyone has an opinion.

"What do you think of Shanny playing RG3 like this?" my agent texted during the Seahawks game.

"I think it's like the main character in the movie *Limitless*," I replied. "He knows the pills are going to run out, but he can't stop taking the pills." There's no denying that there has been something magical about having Griffin on the field . . . but how magical can he be on one leg? And what role is James Andrews playing on the sidelines? Is he a Redskins employee or an emissary of Griffin himself? The issue has shed light on the murky ethics of NFL sideline medicine, where often the well-being of the patient is ignored in favor of the well-being of the club.

Even less-than-mainstream media outlets like the cleverer-than-thou *Slate* got into the RG3 commentary act, writing, "In the minds of the men on the field and the ones on the sidelines wearing headsets, this was not medical malpractice. It was playoff football."[2]

The *USA Today* piece went on to explain that Andrews "remains worried about Griffin's health" and has "been a nervous wreck letting him come back as quick as he has."[3] Which begs the question: Who has ultimate jurisdiction over an injured player's participation? The player or the team doctor . . . or, in this case, the high-end surgeon-to-the-stars brought in to evaluate the player? By pulling on his helmet and trotting back out onto the field in Baltimore, Griffin seemed to have usurped them all. Such is the power of a young icon. Boobie Miles had the same kind of sway over his coaches and advisers. Such is the pressure to perform and stay iconic.

For the first time all season, Griffin seemed a little defensive in press conferences, insisting that he was just "executing the game plan" and that he could do what the Redskins asked of him. There was the sense that he wasn't telling us something. There was the sense that he had probably suffered torn ligaments against Baltimore but was playing any-way. In a world of immediate answers and high-tech medical equipment at each and every NFL stadium, there was no talk of a Griffin MRI until after the playoff game. That seemed strange. But then again, an MRI might provide an answer that nobody wants to hear.

At the same time, there were a gaggle of breathless articles written about Griffin's takeover of the DC metro area. "[Griffin is] uniting dem-ocrats and conservatives," said Mitt Romney in a video clip on Fox.[4] *The Week* gushed that RG3 is "feared by opponents, venerated by team-mates, and beloved by fans," and "has become the biggest celebrity in Washington" in a piece that suggested that Griffin's quarterbacking usurped Obama's reelection in the consciousness of our nation's capital.[5] Even the Fox pregame package had the obligatory "captured the imagi-nation" montage in which DC yuppies, soldiers, barbers, and bus drivers were interviewed about Griffin's impact on the city and on their emo-tions. There was a piece about how Griffin "hates his knee brace" and has threatened to "rip it off" during the game if it becomes obtrusive. It sounded like typical young, tough-guy, "I'm invincible" bluster.

It was odd, then, given the injury controversy above, that Griffin passed the Redskins to a 14-0 lead over Seattle in the first quarter. The first few drives were a run-game clinic, with the line zone-blocking and Alfred Morris running wild over Seattle's defense; but both drives ended with touchdown passes—first to backup running back Evan Royster, and later to backup tight end Logan Paulsen. Seattle head coach Pete Carroll said, "RGIII is real, and Alfred Morris is legit."[6] Against all logic, and on one leg, Griffin appeared to be getting it done. After his second touchdown pass, the Redskins were outgaining Seattle 104 yards to -2 in the first quarter. They ended the quarter with 129 yards, but would only gain 74 more the rest of the game.

Still, those initial drives revealed cracks. Shanahan continued to call designed runs for Griffin, and runs that in previous weeks would have been 15-20 yards instead saw Griffin hobbling out of bounds not unlike Joe Namath near the end of his career. On a few occasions he fell awkwardly or was hit on the knee.

The Redskins got another break in the second half when, after a long clock-grinding drive, Seattle running back Marshawn Lynch coughed up the football. However, Lynch would redeem himself later, bulling his way into the end zone with two Redskins hanging on his back, and Wilson would do his best RG3 impersonation in the second half, exploding up the field on long scrambles that broke the back of the Washington defense.

Though Griffin was clearly hurting, he argued to be kept in the game. "He said, 'Hey, trust me. I want to be in there, and I deserve to be in there,'" Shanahan said. "I couldn't disagree with him."[7] If he'd escaped unscathed, and the Redskins had held on to win, we'd be talking about what a gritty, career-defining performance it was. Instead, after the Lynch touchdown, Griffin's season ended and the controversy began. Griffin bent to try to retrieve a bad shotgun snap, and his knee buckled awkwardly. Griffin grabbed the limb and was hurting so badly that he didn't even try to reach for the ball. Griffin went down without an opposing player even touching him.

Griffin lay on the chewed-up brown turf (also blamed by some for the injury) and was soon surrounded by Redskins medical staff, on the outskirts of which stood Dr. Andrews, the only member of that circle not covered head to toe with Redskins gear. Andrews's only nod to team loyalty was the burgundy-and-gold toboggan he used to keep his head warm on a cold night. In postgame media he would be referred to as a Redskins "consultant."

"It was hard to watch RG3 tonight," said Seattle coach Pete Carroll afterward. "It was hard on him. He was freaking gallant."[8] His Seahawks prevailed 24-14, and with that, Robert Griffin III's rookie season was over.

There would be many press conferences and interviews. There would be an MRI that revealed partial ligament tears. There would be another flight to see Dr. Andrews at his practice in Florida. There would be a defiant Tweet in which Griffin wrote, "Many may question, criticize, & think they have the right answers. But few have been in the line of fire in battle."[9]

There would be a verdict, finally, that Griffin had indeed sustained tears to his ACL and LCL and would need to undergo full reconstructive surgery. His opponent in the Wild Card game, Russell Wilson, would be one of the first to Tweet his support and prayers to Griffin, saying, "May God continue to bless you."[10]

We don't get to choose our final or most profound memories of people, because in this day alone there have been hundreds of different portrayals of Robert Griffin III. There will be many, many more. But the one that I choose to reflect on is the picture of Griffin walking off the field with his arm around his head coach. I choose this because it is a picture of the battle, and it's a portrayal of the bond that forms in battle. Whether Shanahan mishandled the Griffin injury is immaterial in this situation. In this picture they are two men who share a bond because of what they're going through. This is what I choose to remember, and celebrate, about the game of football. It's what those of us who are on the outside will never fully understand and appreciate.

But as I walk away from the NFL playoffs, there is a tinge of nostalgia already. I'll miss my immersion in NFL quarterbacking and I'll miss *this* version of Robert Griffin III, because next year's version will be a year older, a year less exuberant, a year more wary of media and fans. This is the way of life in professional sports. I'm hopeful for what he'll continue to do for the game, as he seems to have taken giant leaps toward legitimizing the running quarterback as a viable, multifaceted NFL weapon. As his young receivers develop, and as his ability to read defenses improves, it's scary to think what a player with his mobility and arm talent can accomplish.

Off the field, he's clearly been given an incredible measure of charisma and interpersonal skill. He has an ability to draw people in, inspire people, and lead his teammates. He may have more natural charisma than any elite quarterback who has come before him—certainly more than any Christian quarterback. As the Redskins continue to win, as subsequent contracts get bigger, and as his fame increases, will his teammates continue to love and respond to him, or will there be division and jealousy? And how does the Christian quarterback honor and glorify God in this context?

In the third chapter of John, we see John the Baptist blazing a trail across Judea like a shooting star. All eyes were on this prophet, who preached and baptized in the name of Christ. Then, eventually, the crowd surged *past* John the Baptist, toward Jesus, his replacement. John's disciples, understandably, were confused and asked him how he felt about it. "He must increase, I must decrease," was John's joyful reply. So how is God glorified as man is doing his best to glorify an NFL quarterback? My hope is that Griffin's tenure will show us something of how this is possible.

And whether Robert Griffin III takes the NFL by storm, or whether he underwhelms long-term because of injury or some other reason, I'll remember his rookie year fondly. And I'll miss it, because he'll never be new again.

APPENDIX A

POSTSEASON QUARTERBACK RANKING

I revisited my ranking of every starting quarterback in the league (in Week 8) that appeared in the chapter entitled "A Grown Man's Game." Below is the postseason revision.

THE HALL OF FAME TIER

Tom Brady, Patriots. This could have easily been Peyton Manning, who is putting on a quarterbacking clinic this season.

Peyton Manning, Broncos. Could have easily been Tom Brady, who is still consistently amazing and seems to be the one constant amidst personnel changes in New England.

Aaron Rodgers, Packers. Over 4,200 yards, 49 touchdowns, and only 8 picks. Rodgers is a surgeon who at only twenty-nine still has significant upside. Scary to think what he'd do with a running game.

Drew Brees, Saints. Still a statistical animal (over 5,200 astonishing yards), even though his team disappointed him this season.

THE "YOUNG AND SENSATIONAL" TIER

Andrew Luck, Colts. Set a rookie record for passing yards in a season, is already a sophisticated reader of defenses, and is still a good enough athlete to run when he needs to (which isn't often). Luck gets the nod over RG3 (barely) only because his style will age better.

Robert Griffin III, Redskins. Was as big a sensation to hit this league, on and off the field, as any player in recent memory. Griffin was stunningly accurate and stunningly wise with the football for a rookie. Perhaps most impressive was his team leadership.

Matt Ryan, Falcons. Matty Ice is getting it done statistically (his best season yet), and is piloting an offense loaded with weapons. Has already played in two Pro Bowls.

Russell Wilson, Seahawks. His passing numbers are consistent with the rest of this tier (also, incidentally, better than Cutler's), and he added almost 500 yards and 4 touchdowns on the ground. If this was a year devoid of Andrew Luck and RG3, Wilson would be the sensational story of the year.

Colin Kaepernick, 49ers. Kappy is a Griffin/Vick-type runner (nearly 500 yards in 7 games) and a scary good passer, hitting over 60 percent with 10 TDs and just 3 picks. Can you say freakish upside? I questioned Harbaugh for benching Alex Smith, but at the same time I can absolutely see why he did it. He's ranked this high because he plays on a good team with a creative coach and a great offensive line.

THE "ROETHLISBERGER" TIER

Ben Roethlisberger, Steelers. Had a Roethlisberger-esque year, which is to say pretty doggone good but not statistically dominant, while his team underperformed around him. He drops because as I look at the list above, I think I'd rather have any of the young guys (all of whom, incidentally, are in the playoffs) than Big Ben at this point. And for the first time in his career, his supporting cast has significant question marks.

Eli Manning, Giants. Is ranked above Rivers and Romo because he's won Super Bowls and is ranked below the aforementioned young guys because they were all better than Eli this year; and I don't think we've yet seen the best of what they can do (whereas we have seen the best of what Eli can do). Is he elite? No, but he's still very good.

THE "PHILIP RIVERS" TIER

Philip Rivers, Chargers. I was ready to put Rivers in the "Overrated but Still Employed" Tier but then realized how much better he was, statistically, than Cutler. The presence of Rivers in San Diego makes it an attractive job opportunity for a prospective coach.

Tony Romo, Cowboys. Romo redeemed himself and probably saved his job with a strong second half of the season in which he drastically cut down on turnovers and seemed to find his groove. Still, look for Dallas to draft or acquire a project QB to develop for the future.

THE "HIGH-END GAME MANAGERS" TIER

Matt Schaub, Texans. Schaub can play. He knows what he has (Arian Foster in the backfield, a great defense, and Andre Johnson) and knows how to use it.

Alex Smith, 49ers/Chiefs. Consider this: Smith was having a great season (70 percent completions, 13 TDs, 5 INTs) before he got Wally-Pipped by Colin Kaepernick. He's only twenty-eight and will be Kansas City's starting quarterback next season.

Joe Flacco, Ravens. I can't shake the feeling that Flacco is only as good as the parts around him, and as those parts go, so goes Flacco. All that to say, I'm not sure he can win games on his own.

THE "YOUNG AND SLIGHTLY
LESS SENSATIONAL" TIER

Andy Dalton, Bengals. Dalton almost made the "Young and Sensational" Tier, is piloting a talented young offense with weapons like A. J. Green and Jermaine Gresham, and passed the Bengals into the play-offs. Honestly, if I were starting a team today and had a choice between Dalton and Flacco, I'd take Dalton in a heartbeat.

Cam Newton, Panthers. Like Stafford, he's stuck in organizational limbo with limited talent around him. His completion percentage, yardage, and touchdowns all took a dip this season.

Matthew Stafford, Lions. Upside: Stafford's main weapon, Calvin Johnson, is the best receiver in pro football. Downside: The rest of his organization, from the coach on down, is an absolute train wreck. Stafford may never fully realize his potential, and his stats took a nose-dive this season. Still, if I had to start a franchise with anyone in this tier, it would be Stafford because he's the best pure passer. He's ranked this low because of the aforementioned organizational gong-show he finds himself in.

THE "OVERRATED BUT STILL EMPLOYED" TIER

Jay Cutler, Bears. On one hand, Cutler is the best and most talented quarterback Chicago has had since Jim McMahon, and honestly maybe since Sid Luckman, which may say more about Chicago's dearth of quarterbacking talent than Cutler's actual ability. He still zeroes in on Brandon Marshall way too much and still makes way too many mistakes. Consider the fact that Cutler's numbers were significantly worse than those of Carson Palmer (Raiders) and Ryan Fitzpatrick (Bills), who are probably both on their way to backup jobs next season. It does beg the question, "Why do we still think of Jay Cutler as a star?" I'm inclined to think that Jay Cutler is a year or two away from being Carson Palmer.

THE "YOUNG BUT LIMITED" TIER

Sam Bradford, Rams. His completion percentage lingers just under 60 percent, which is a little worrisome, but he may still flourish under Jeff Fisher's tutelage.

Josh Freeman, Bucs. His great 2010 looks more like a statistical aberration than the statistical norm. The Bucs were back to being bad, and Freeman's completion percentage dipped down to 54 percent this season. Still, I think I'd rather have Freeman than anyone below him on this list. But I'd rather have Bradford than Freeman.

Ryan Tannehill, Dolphins. Tannehill's numbers are a lot like Bradford's and Weeden's, which is to say decent but not great.

Christian Ponder, Vikings. Ponder's job is to hand the football to Adrian Peterson, and secondarily, to be good when Minnesota needs him to be, which as it turns out isn't very often (see: Peterson).

Nick Foles, Eagles. Played pretty well considering that his coach was a lame duck and much of his team gave up down the stretch. Foles is a big kid with a big arm.

Brandon Weeden, Browns. You know what's weird? Weeden is a year older than Alex Smith, who seems like he's been quarterbacking in San Francisco for, oh, forever. I'd much rather have Smith than Weeden at this point. Weeden has shown flashes, but he needs to learn to read the field better, and organizational upheaval makes him a question mark. He's looking like a first-round reach.

Jake Locker, Titans. I still believe in Locker, but he needs to play in an offense (similar to RG3) that is calibrated to play to his strengths and make him successful. That's not happening yet in Tennessee. The same thing that plagued him in college (completion percentage) is plaguing him with the Titans, and he's having shoulder surgery this offseason. He's got another year, tops, to prove he can get the job done, and Munchak's job probably depends on his development.

THE "PROBABLY ON THEIR WAY OUT" TIER

Carson Palmer, Raiders. I revisited his production, and he played a lot better than I thought—holding things down as his offense's only star, Darren McFadden, continued to be hurt and overrated. Palmer isn't a star in this league, but he's not bad, and he's probably better than the last four guys in the previous tier.

Mike Vick, Eagles. A lack of production and a nasty concussion paved the way for Nick Foles in Philadelphia, though the hiring of former Oregon coach Chip Kelly seems as if it might give Vick a new lease on NFL life.

Ryan Fitzpatrick, Bills. Again, like Palmer, didn't play badly but doesn't (and won't) excite the fan base. But is there anyone at the quarterback position in the 2013 Draft who will excite the fan base? Fitz could keep his job by default.

Blaine Gabbert, Jaguars. Like Joey Harrington, Gabbert was a player with potential who unfortunately was drafted into a horrible situation. Gabbert is 5-19 as a starter, and we may never know how good (or bad) he actually is because he plays for Jacksonville.

Mark Sanchez, Jets. His numbers were dreadful this season, but do me a favor and name a starting wide receiver for the New York Jets (crickets chirping). His coach, Rex Ryan, should have been fired and is oddly loyal to Sanchez, who could parlay that loyalty into another season as a starter in New York. I thought both Sanchez and Ryan would be gone, and was wrong on both accounts.

THE "DEFINITELY ON THEIR WAY OUT" TIER

Matt Cassel and Brady Quinn, Chiefs. Quinn received the several opportunities that seem to come standard with a first-round draft choice, and he appears to have done very little with them. I believed in Quinn's abilities coming out of Notre Dame . . . and still want to, but I think I've missed on this prospect. Cassel was a backup at USC and began his NFL career as a backup in New England. He'll be a backup again soon, as Kansas City has traded for Alex Smith.

Kevin Kolb and Ryan Lindley and John Skelton, Cardinals. Arizona will have a complete overhaul in the offseason, starting with the quarterback position.

APPENDIX B

FOOTBALL GLOSSARY

B elow is a short and basic glossary of some of the terms I use frequently on the preceding pages.

Cover Three: In this defensive coverage scheme, the two corners and free safety each have responsibility for a deep third of the field, while the strong safety plays like a linebacker. Cover Three is a great run-stopping defense because the strong safety can move up into the "box" and act as another linebacker because the corners never have their backs to the play. Cover Three is sound against deep passes, but vulnerable against the short passing game.

Cover Two: A defensive coverage scheme pioneered by Bud Carson's Steeler defenses of the 1970s and modified by Tony Dungy's Buccaneer defenses in the late '90s (Tampa-2), this defense is characterized by the two deep safeties each taking a deep "half" of the field in coverage.

Dig Route: An intermediate pass pattern in which the receiver runs straight down the field before breaking inside and running across the middle.

Free Safety: A defensive back, the free safety usually aligns opposite the tight end and is the lighter and faster of the two safeties. His primary responsibility is to help the cornerback to his side on pass plays. Baltimore Raven Ed Reed is the current gold standard for NFL free safeties.

Fullback: Traditionally an important figure in the West Coast offense, the big, bulky, lead blocker is becoming something of a relic in today's NFL. However, the Redskins used fullback Darrel Young effectively as a receiver out of the backfield.

Left Tackle: The most valuable player on the offensive line, charged with protecting the quarterback's blind side, the left tackle has become one of the most sought-after and highly compensated positions in the NFL draft each year. Incidentally, the book *The Blind Side* is as much about the development of this position as it is about the feel-good story of a black kid growing up in a white family.

Out Route: A pass pattern in which the receiver runs straight down the field and breaks outside, toward the sideline.

Outside Linebacker: This is the defense's edge rusher, the player whose job it is to challenge the left tackle and produce quarterback sacks and pressure for the defenses. Examples of elite outside backers include DeMarcus Ware, Clay Matthews Jr., and Aldon Smith. Hall of Famer Lawrence Taylor provided the prototype for this position in the 1980s.

Pistol Formation: Pioneered by University of Nevada coach Chris Ault, the pistol is like the shotgun with a shorter snap (2–3 yards), sometimes a tailback behind the quarterback, with more versatility. Teams who run the pistol have a greater diversity of run plays (power plays, counters, etc.) than do their traditional shotgun counterparts. San Francisco rode the pistol formation and Colin Kaepernick to a

Super Bowl appearance. Mike Shanahan and RG3 also used the pistol with great effectiveness this season.

Play-Action: Refers to a play in which the quarterback fakes a handoff to the running back and then drops back to pass. This concept is meant to "freeze" the linebackers and safeties, giving receivers time to get behind the coverage and get open. The vast majority of RG3's successful downfield throws happened off of play-action.

Post Route: A pass pattern in which the receiver runs straight upfield for 10–12 yards, then breaks at an angle across the middle, toward the goalpost—hence the name "post."

Seam Route: A pass pattern in which the receiver (usually a tight end or slot receiver) runs straight upfield in an area outside the tackles but inside the yard markers that adorn the field. New England's tight end, Rob Gronkowski, with his unique size and speed, is especially effective running in the seam.

Shotgun Formation: Popularized in the 1990s, the shotgun features the quarterback lined up four yards behind the center and is intended to give the quarterback more time in the pocket by alleviating his dropback and creating greater visibility by putting him farther away from tall offensive and defensive linemen. Several teams, like Washington, Seattle, and San Francisco, operated out of the shotgun as their primary offensive formation in 2012. For the sake of perspective, consider the fact that Hall of Fame 49ers quarterback Steve Young didn't run *one* play out of the shotgun in his entire career.

Skinny Post: This pass pattern is sort of a happy medium between a post and a "go" route, in which the receiver runs a post, but runs it at a "skinnier" angle, meaning that his break to the post is not as drastic.

Slant: A short, quick route in which the receiver takes a couple of hard steps off the line of scrimmage and then breaks inside on a shallow angle. The quarterback takes a quick, three-step drop and fires a laser to the slanting receiver. Joe Montana and Jerry Rice made the slant into an art form in Bill Walsh's West Coast offense.

Spread Offense: The spread is an offensive set that features four, and sometimes five, wide receivers, no fullback or tight end, and often a mobile quarterback operating primarily out of a shotgun formation. But it's more than a formation—it's a philosophy. The spread—often an up-tempo, no-huddle offense—has taken the high school and college game by storm and now, via Griffin and players like Russel Wilson and Colin Kaepernick, is making its presence felt in the pro game.

Strong Safety: Of the two safeties, the strong safety usually aligns on the tight end side of the formation and is often the bigger and more physical of the two in order to be more effective in run support. Prototypical strong safeties include former Bronco Steve Atwater and current Steeler Troy Polamalu.

Tight End: Part lineman, part receiver, this player needs to be big, fast, and versatile since today's NFL tight end has become a key weapon. Atlanta's Tony Gonzales has been and still is the Rolls-Royce of the tight end position.

West Coast Offense: Pioneered and popularized by legendary 49ers head coach Bill Walsh and his coaching protégés (including Mike Holmgren, Andy Reid, and Mike Shanahan), the West Coast offense is really just a catchall term for an offense that utilizes a short, rhythm passing game (meaning lots of three-step drops and quarterbacks throwing to a spot) and lots of receivers in the pattern as a means of controlling the football. When pro football was still dominated by semi-archaic, Parcells-style, run-heavy offenses in the 1980s, the Walsh offense and all of its subsequent variants changed offensive football forever.

Zone Blocking: Mike Shanahan may not have invented zone blocking, but he perfected it as Denver's head coach, where his teams routinely put up monster seasons running the football. In the zone scheme, instead of blocking a man, linemen step to a "space," and the running back's job is to run with his linemen, make one cut upfield, and find the "crease" in the defense. Linemen who excel in this scheme are typically a little smaller and more agile.

APPENDIX C

PLAY AND FORMATION DIAGRAMS

Cover 2 Defense:

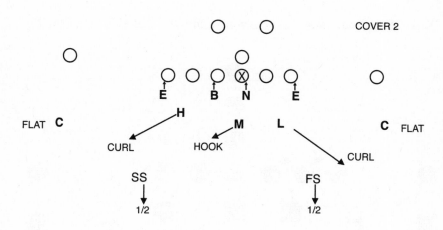

Cover 3 Defense:

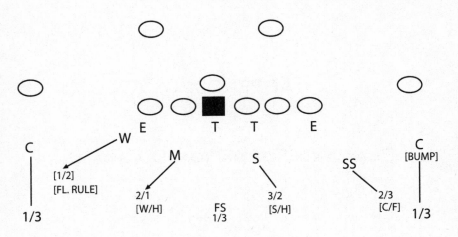

The Dick LeBeau Steeler 3-4 Defense (the one that shut down RG3):

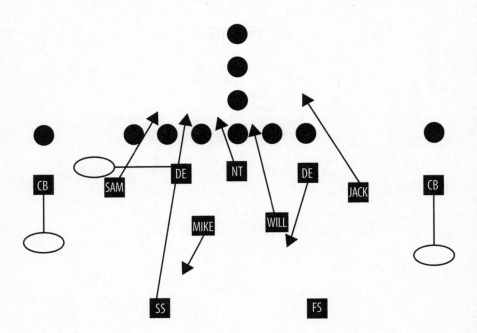

Shotgun Zone Read (the bread-and-butter RG3 running play):

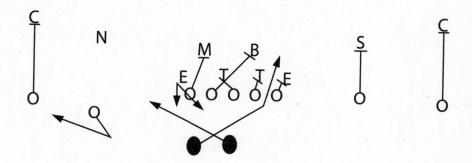

Pistol Formation Read Option (another 'Skins staple):

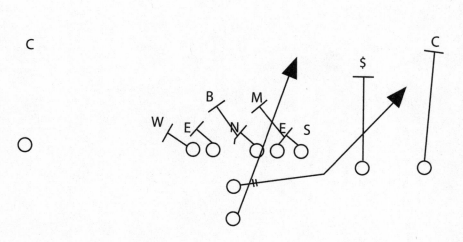

NOTES

Chapter 1. Nobody Gets Famous by Accident: Creating Robert Griffin III

1. Robert Griffin III, Twitter posts, November 11, 2012, http://twitter.com/RGIII.

2. *The Marinovich Project*, directed by John Dorsey and Andrew Stephan (2011; ESPN *30 for 30* series).

3. Rich Campbell, "RG3's Traits Passed Down from Father," *Washington Times*, November 21, 2012, http://www.washingtontimes.com/news/2012/nov/21/rg3s-traits-passed-down-from-father/?page=all.

4. Rich Campbell, "More on Robert Griffin III and His Relationship with His Father," *Washington Times*, November 26, 2012, http://www.washingtontimes.com/blog/redskins-watch/2012/nov/26/more-robert-griffin-iii-and-his-relationship-his-f.

5. Ibid.

6. Ibid.

7. Copperas Cove, Texas High School Football Program, Copperas Cove Football, accessed February 25, 2012, http://www.covefootball.com.

8. Evan Sharpley, in discussion with the author, October 2012.

9. Associated Press, "Griffin Accounts for 4 TDs as Baylor Trounces Texas," ESPN.com, December 3, 2011, accessed February 26, 2013, http://scores.espn.go.com/ncf/recap?gameId=313370239.

10. Ibid.

11. Ibid.

12. "Breaking Down Heisman Trophy Financials: Baylor Estimates $250M Boost After RGIII's Win," *Sports Business Daily*, December 7, 2012,

http://m.sportsbusinessdaily.com/Daily/Issues/2012/12/07/Marketing
-and-Sponsorship/Heisman.aspx.

13. Elizabeth McGarr, "Art Briles: On Advising RG3 and the Building of the Campus's Future," SI.com, August 16, 2012, http://sportsillustrated.cnn .com/vault/article/magazine/MAG1203446/index.htm.

14. Terry Shea, in discussion with the author, October 2012.

15. Ibid.

16. Ibid.

17. Ibid.

18. Ibid.

19. Ibid.

Chapter 2. From Bobby Douglass to Timothy Tebow to RG3: A Brief History of Running Quarterbacks

1. All stats to follow courtesy of www.pro-football-reference.com.

2. David Fleming, "With a Bullet," *ESPN The Magazine*, April 16, 2001, accessed August 16, 2012, http://espn.go.com/magazine/vol4no08vick .html.

3. Ibid.

4. "Top Ten Mobile QB's: Randall Cunningham," NFL.com, accessed February 28, 2013, http://www.nfl.com/videos/nfl-game-highlights /09000d5d801f9a2e/Top-Ten-Mobile-QBs-Randall-Cunningham.

5. Chris Connelly (reporter), "E:60—Randall Cunningham," E:60 Special, ESPN.com, November 8, 2011, http://espn.go.com/video/clip?id=7208355.

6. Richard Glazer, "The Selling of Superback Randall Cunningham," *Football Digest*, January 1990, 48–54.

7. A sports agent, in discussion with the author, November 2012.

8. Pat Kirwan, "Running Quarterbacks Revolutionizing Game, but Not Ready to Win It All Yet," CBSSports.com, July 24, 2012, http://www .cbssports.com/nfl/story/19648820/running-quarterbacks-revolutionizing -game-but-not-ready-to-win-it-all-yet.

9. Jim Kelly, in discussion with the author, November 2012.

10. "Draft Prospect—Robert Griffin III," ProFootballWeekly.com, accessed July 24, 2012, http://www.profootballweekly.com/prospects/player/robert -griffin-iii-10.

11. John Keim, "Redskins QB Robert Griffin III Flexes Leadership Skills," CBSSports.com, November 1, 2012, http://www.cbssports.com/nfl/blog /nfl-rapidreports/20777790/redskins-qb-robert-griffin-iii-flexes -leadership-skills.

12. Rick Maese, "NFL draft: Robert Griffin III Embarks on Pro Career, and Washington Redskins Fans Await," *Washington Post*, April 21, 2012, http://www.washingtonpost.com/sports/nfl-draft-robert-griffin-iii -embarks-on-pro-career-and-washington-redskins-fans-await/2012/04/21 /gIQAv39dYT_story.html.

Chapter 3. Pro Day and the Inexact Science of NFL Scouting

1. 2006 Central Michigan Chippewas Media Guide, accessed May 24, 2013, http://www.cmuchippewas.com/ViewArticle.dbml?DB_OEM_ID =10500&ATCLID=528049, 9.
2. Ibid, 13.
3. Ian Rapoport, "RG3 Grabs Control of Destiny by Declining Colts' Workout Request," NFL.com, April 3, 2012, http://www.nfl.com/draft /story/09000d5d8280ff92/article/rg3-grabs-control-of-destiny-by -declining-colts-workout-request.
4. Ibid.
5. CapitolPunishmentDMV (YouTube user), "Robert Griffin III's Pro Day—Full Workout and Interview (3-21-2012)," YouTube.com, uploaded March 22, 2012, http://www.youtube.com/watch?v=bXMxwoi7k6I.
6. Ibid.
7. Glenn Guilbeau, "Russell Wows Scouts at LSU's Pro Day" *USA Today*, updated March 15, 2007, http://usatoday30.usatoday.com/sports/football /draft/2007-03-15-russell-pro-day_N.htm?csp=34.

Chapter 4. The Hotter the Heat, the Harder the Steel: Selling Robert Griffin III

1. EvoShield (YouTube user), "RG3 Welcomes You to #EvoArmy," YouTube .com, uploaded August 20, 2012, http://www.youtube.com/watch?v=iBu1 xcTp8zc&feature=share&list=UUELX5EC2YYyvFxzZJy5lGeA.
2. Eugene Lee, in discussion with the author, November 2012.
3. Ibid.
4. CapitolPunishmentDMV (YouTube user), "Gruden's QB Camp: Robert Griffin III (Full Show)," YouTube.com, uploaded April 3, 2012, http:// www.youtube.com/watch?v=N-_DYkYkidA. Originally aired on ESPN on April 2, 2012.
5. Lance Madden, "Robert Griffin III, Adidas Have a Lot of Sock Swag," *Forbes*, September 21, 2012, http://www.forbes.com/sites/lancemadden /2012/09/21/robert-griffin-iii-adidas-have-a-lot-of-sock-swag.
6. Chris Chase, "Robert Griffin III Gave Socks to Trick-or-Treaters," *USA*

Today, November 1, 2012, http://www.usatoday.com/story/gameon
/2012/11/01/robert-griffin-iii-rgiii-socks-halloween/1674457.

Chapter 5. What the Redskins Needed Was Quarterbacking

1. *Pro Football Hall of Fame*, Sonny Jurgensen profile, accessed May 24, 2013, http://www.profootballhof.com/hof/member.aspx?player_id=111.
2. Terry Shea, *Eyes Up: Coaching the Men with the Nerve to Play the Most Challenging Position in Football* (Leawood, KS: Shea Publishing, 2011) 277-278.
3. Peter King, "The 1-2 Punch," SIVault.com, April 23, 2012, http:// sportsillustrated.cnn.com/vault/article/magazine/MAG1197389/index.htm.
4. Shea, *Eyes Up*, 279.
5. Ibid.
6. King, "The 1-2 Punch."
7. Stephen Wyche, "Redskins' Mike Shanahan: Taking RG3 is Nearly a Sure Thing," NFL.com, updated August 3, 2012, http://www.nfl.com/draft /story/09000d5d8289631c/article/redskins-mike-shanahan-taking-rg3-is -nearly-a-sure-thing.
8. Mark Maske, "NFL Draft 2012: Redskins Make Robert Griffin III Official," *Washington Post*, April 26, 2012, http://articles.washingtonpost .com/2012-04-26/sports/35450744_1_luck-and-griffin-robert-griffin-iii -nfl-draft.
9. Zennie62 (YouTube user), "RG3 Dad Robert Griffin II—A Frank Talk About How His Son Was Raised," YouTube.com, uploaded December 9, 2012, http://www.youtube.com/watch?v=bRaCUQuVLQo.
10. Brian Billick and Michael MacCambridge, *More Than a Game: The Glorious Present and Uncertain Future of the NFL* (New York, NY: Scribner, 2012), 76.
11. BallsHogRadio (YouTube user), "Redskins Fans Welcome RG3 to DC and Erupt when Draft Pick is Announced!" YouTube.com, uploaded August 27, 2012, http://www.youtube.com/watch?v=gfO4GVO-R64.
12. Jason La Canfora, "RG3's just starting but already winning over his own locker room," CBSSports.com, July 26, 2012, http://www.cbssports.com /nfl/story/19663627/rg3s-just-starting-but-already-winning-over-his-own -locker-room.
13. Maske, "NFL Draft 2012."

Chapter 6. Robert Griffin III Is Sensational
(But So Is Kyle Shanahan)

1. John Clayton, "Robert Griffin III Passes Eye Test," ESPN.com, August 1, 2012, http://espn.go.com/nfl/trainingcamp12/story/_/page/claytoncamp skins120801/nfl-observations-washington-redskins-training-camp.
2. Jason La Canfora, "RG3's Just Starting but Already Winning over His Own Locker Room," CBSSports.com, July 26, 2012, http://www.cbssports.com/ nfl/story/19663627/rg3s-just-starting-but-already-winning-over-his-own -locker-room.
3. Ibid.
4. Ibid.
5. Ibid.
6. Ibid.
7. Ibid.
8. Ibid.

Chapter 7. Warriors and Humans: On Injury,
Marcus Lattimore, and RG3

1. Associated Press, "RG3 Drives Washington Redskins, then Billy Cundiff Boots Tampa Bay Bucs," NFL.com, September 30, 2012, http://www.nfl .com/news/story/0ap1000000067855/article/rg3-drives-washington -redskins-then-billy-cundiff-boots-tampa-bay-bucs.
2. Ibid.
3. Kimberly Jones, "Alfread Morris Is Washington Redskins' Other Standout Rookie," NFL.com, October 19, 2012, http://www.nfl.com/news/story /0ap1000000082322/printable/alfred-morris-is-washington-redskins -iotheri-standout-rookie.
4. Ibid.
5. Ibid.
6. Andrew Seligman, "Urlacher Says Again He'd Lie about Concussion," *New York Times*, November 15, 2012, http://nytimes.stats.com/fb/story .asp?i=20121115134619457337908&ref=hea&tm=&src=.
7. Will Brinson, "NFL Sends Memo to Teams on New Concussion Policy," CBSSports.com, December 22, 2011, http://www.cbssports.com/mcc /blogs/entry/22475988/33991446.
8. Ibid.

9. SwizZzStudio (YouTube user), "2013 Outback Bowl: Michigan Wolverines vs. South Carolina Gamecocks (Full Game)," uploaded January 5, 2013, http://www.youtube.com/watch?v=SiC0XYxP6F4.

10. Ibid.

11. Robert Griffin III, Twitter post, October 27, 2012, http://twitter.com /RGIII.

Chapter 8. Fight for Old Dixie: A Brief Racial History of the Washington Redskins

1. Associated Press, "RG3's 76-Yard Scamper Seals Washington Redskins' Win Over Minnesota Vikings," NFL.com, October 14, 2012, http://www .nfl.com/news/story/0ap1000000080289/article/rg3s-76yard-scamper -seals-washington-redskins-win-over-minnesota-vikings.

2. Ibid.

3. Thomas G. Smith, *Showdown: JFK and the Integration of the Washington Redskins* (Boston, MA: Beacon Press, 2011).

4. Robert Littal, "Robert Griffin III Buys His Fiancée Rebecca Liddicoat a Bentley, Maybe," BlackSportsOnline.com, April 30, 2012, http:// blacksportsonline.com/home/2012/04/robert-griffin-iii-buys-his -fiancee-rebecca-liddicoat-a-bentley.

5. StephanMyzel (YouTube user), "Skip Bayless, Stephen A. Smith & Rob Parker on RG3 'Cornball Brother' Full Pt. 1," YouTube, uploaded December 17, 2012, http://www.youtube.com/watch?v=PdQL4aRSjPI. Originally aired on ESPN2.

6. Ibid.

7. Smith, *Showdown*, 212.

8. Fredkiz (YouTube user), "Doug Williams Breaking the Barrier ESPN 2013," uploaded February 3, 2013, http://www.youtube.com/watch?v =XyYdWw6f4Pw.

9. Jim Corbett, "Robert Griffin's Dad Responds to Rob Parker," *USA Today*, December 13, 2012, http://www.usatoday.com/story/sports/nfl /redskins/2012/12/13/robert-griffin-iii-washington-redskins -rob-parker/1768501.

Chapter 9. A Grown Man's Game: Robert Griffin III Is Human

1. "A Little More RG3," Fox Sports video, 2:20, November 12, 2012, msn.foxsports.com/lacesout/a-little-more-rg3.

2. "Redskins: Wednesday Quote Machine—Mike Shanahan, Robert Griffin III; Pittsburgh Steelers Mike Tomlin; Ben Roethlisberger," Viva Loudoun, October 25, 2012, http://vivaloudoun.blogspot.com/2012/10/redskins-wednesday-quote-machine-mike.html.

3. "A Little More RG," Fox Sports.

4. "Redskins: Wednesday Quote Machine," Viva Loudoun.

5. Ibid.

6. Ibid.

7. LeBron James, Twitter post, November 22, 2012, http://twitter.com/KingJames.

8. "Redskins: Wednesday Quote Machine," Viva Loudoun.

9. Ibid.

10. Associated Press, "Pittsburgh Steelers Shut Down Washington Redskins and Robert Griffin III," NFL.com, October 28, 2012, http://m.nfl.com/news/0ap1000000086580/pittsburgh-steelers-shut-down-washington-redskins-and-robert-griffin-iii.

11. Ibid.

12. "Redskins: Wednesday Quote Machine," Viva Loudoun.

13. Doug Farrar, "Cam Newton's Attitude Didn't Win Him Any Friends at the Pro Bowl," Yahoo! Sports, December 5, 2012, http://sports.yahoo.com/blogs/nfl-shutdown-corner/cam-newton-attitude-didn-t-win-him-friends-225644136--nfl.html.

14. Dan Steinberg, "DeAngelo Williams Angry at Redskins' 'Homecoming' Game," DC Sports Blog, *Washington Post*, November 4, 2012, http://www.washingtonpost.com/blogs/dc-sports-bog/wp/2012/11/04/deangelo-williams-angry-at-redskins-homecoming-game.

15. *Jon Gruden's Quarterback Camp*, http://search.espn.go.com/gruden-qb-camp/.

16. Larry Brown, "Jimmy Johnson: RGIII Is MVP of NFL," FoxSports.com, November 22, 2012, http://msn.foxsports.com/lacesout/jimmy-johnson-rg3-is-mvp-of-nfl/.

17. Mark Maske, "Loss to Panthers Has Coach Mike Shanahan Looking to the Future," *Washington Post*, November 3, 2012, http://articles.washingtonpost.com/2012-11-04/sports/35503286_1_playoff-spot-football-team-linebacker-lorenzo-alexander.

18. Mike Wise, "The Redskins Might be Playing to Evaluate Players, but It's Too Early for Mike Shanahan to Say So," *Washington Post*, November 4, 2012, http://articles.washingtonpost.com/2012-11-04/sports/35504209_1_chris-cooley-robert-griffin-iii-football-team.

Chapter 10. God and Quarterbacking: Faith, Prosperity, and Pro Football

1. Chris Moody, "RG3 on Playing Football in a Political Town, His Dream Pick-Up Game with Obama and More: The Yahoo News Interview," Yahoo! News, November 28, 2012, http://news.yahoo.com/blogs/ticket/rg3-playing -football-political-town-dream-pick-game-101516817--election.html.

2. Ibid.

3. Daniel Whyte, "Robert Griffin III: 'My Relationship with God Is My Most Important Influence,'" BCNN1, May 6, 2012, http://www .blackchristiannews.com/news/2012/05/robert-griffin-iii-my-relationship -with-god-is-my-most-important-influence.html.

4. Robert Griffin III, Twitter post, December 9, 2012, http://twitter.com /RGIII.

5. Dr. James Spiegel, in discussion with the author, December 2012.

6. Nate Ulrich, "Video: Transcript from NFL Scouting Combine Q&A with Baylor QB Robert Griffin III," Ohio.com, http://www.ohio.com/blogs /cleveland-browns/cleveland-browns-1.270107/video-transcript-from-nfl -scouting-combine-q-a-with-baylor-qb-robert-griffin-iii-1.272749.

7. UBC, University Baptist Church, accessed February 27, 2013, http:// www.ubcwaco.org.

8. "About Us—What We Believe," University Baptist Church, accessed February 27, 2013, http://www.ubcwaco.org.

9. "UBC: Sacred & Secular," University Baptist Church, accessed February 27, 2013, http://www.ubcwaco.org/about_us/sacred.html.

10. Chad Bonham, "David Crowder Talks Up Baylor's Heisman Winning Quarterback Robert Griffin III," Beliefnet.com, Inspiring Athletes blog, December 2011, http://blog.beliefnet.com/inspiringathletes/2011/12 /david-crowder-talks-up-baylors-heisman-winning-quarterback-robert -griffin-iii.html.

11. Brendan Vaughan, "How to Beat the Draft," GQ, September 2012, http:// www.gq.com/sports/profiles/201209/robert-griffin-rg3-gq-september-2012.

12. Jim Corbett, "Redskins QB Robert Griffin III after big win: God Is on Our Side," USA Today, December 4, 2012, http://www.usatoday.com /story/sports/nfl/2012/12/04/washington-redskins-beat-new-york-giants -17-16-with-robert-griffin-iii-rgiii-rg3/1744745/?utm_source=feedburner &utm_medium=feed&utm_campaign=Feed%3A.

13. Chad Bonham, "A Conversation with Washington Redskins Running Back Roy Helu Jr.," Beliefnet.com, Inspiring Athletes blog, October 2012,

http://blog.beliefnet.com/inspiringathletes/2012/10/a-conversation-with
-washington-redskins-running-back-roy-helu-jr.html.

14. Gregg Rosenthal, "RG3's Washington Redskins Jersey Is NFL's Top
Seller," NFL.com, December 17, 2012, http://www.nfl.com/news/story
/0ap1000000113271/article/rg3s-washington-redskins-jersey-is
-nfls-top-seller.

15. *Baltimore Sun* staff, "Ray Lewis' Full Statement to Media on His
Retirement," *Baltimore Sun*, January 2, 2013, http://articles.baltimoresun.
com/2013-01-02/sports/bal-ray-lewis-full-statement-to-media-on-his
-retirement-20130102_1_ray-lewis-full-ride-scholarship-god.

16. Gregory Gwyn-Williams Jr., "RG3 on Coming to D.C.: 'I Fear God,'"
CNSNews.com, November 30, 2012, http://cnsnews.com/blog/gregory
-gwyn-williams-jr/rg3-coming-dc-i-fear-god.

Chapter 12. Pursuit of Perfection

1. Mark Maske, "Mike Shanahan Addresses Redskins Players about His
Postgame Comments," *Washington Post*, November 6, 2012, http://www
.washingtonpost.com/blogs/football-insider/wp/2012/11/06/mike
-shanahan-addresses-redskins-players-about-his-postgame-comments.

2. Associated Press, "RG3 Has Four TD Passes; Washington Redskins Beat
Philadelphia Eagles," NFL.com, November 18, 2012, http://m.nfl.com
/news/0ap1000000096928/rg3-has-four-td-passes-washington-redskins
-beat-philadelphia-eagles.

3. Rowan Kavner, "Short Week Hasn't Hurt Cowboys on Past Thanksgivings,"
DallasCowboys.com, November 19, 2012, http://www.dallascowboys.com
/news/article-RowanKavner/Short-Week-Hasn't-Hurt-Cowboys-On-Past
-Thanksgivings-/00134c6e-66c2-4b27-b72a-f18b5a7865ab.

4. Trent Dilfer, *The Sports Fix* (radio show), ESPN 980, December 7, 2012.

5. Associated Press, "Robert Griffin III, Washington Redskins Hold Off
Dallas Cowboys' Rally," NFL.com, November 22, 2012, http://www.nfl
.com/news/story/0ap1000000099265/article/robert-griffin-iii-washington
-redskins-hold-off-dallas-cowboys-rally.

6. Ibid.

Chapter 13. Vick, Irony, and Injury

1. Les Bowen, "Vick Comes Full Circle with Eagles: Back to Third-Team
Quarterback," Philly.com, December 19, 2012, http://articles.philly.com
/2012-12-19/sports/35892742_1_nick-foles-michael-vick-vick-s-eagles.

2. Associated Press, "RG3 Injured in Washington Redskins' Comeback over Baltimore Ravens," NFL.com, December 10, 2012, http://www.nfl.com /news/story/0ap1000000108423/article/rg3-injured-in-washington -redskins-comeback-over-baltimore-ravens.

3. Ibid.

4. Ibid.

5. Ibid.

6. Ibid.

7. Brian Tinsman, "Paul Has a Team of Tight End Mentors," Redskins.com, June 8, 2012, http://www.redskins.com/news-and-events/article-1/Paul -Has-A-Team-Of-Tight-End-Mentors/24f67c40-5629-4bcd-886a -f08f442d34c1.

8. Ibid.

9. Ibid.

10. Associated Press, "Kirk Cousins Impresses in Washington Redskins' Victory over Cleveland Browns," NFL.com, December 16, 2012, http:// www.nfl.com/news/story/0ap1000000112122/article/kirk-cousins -impresses-in-washington-redskins-victory-over-cleveland-browns.

11. Ibid.

12. Ibid.

Epilogue. He'll Never Be New Again

1. Robert Klemko, "Dr. James Andrews Says He Never Cleared Robert Griffin III to Go Back after Game Injury," *USA Today*, January 6, 2013, http://www.usatoday.com/story/sports/nfl/redskins/2013/01/06/dr-james -andrews-disputes-coach-mike-shanahans-version-of-washington-redskins -quarterback-robert-griffin-iii-knee-injury/1811689.

2. Josh Levin, "'You Have to Step Up and Be a Man Sometimes': Robert Griffin III Twisted His Knee on the Oldest Clichés in Sport," *Slate*, January 6, 2013, http://www.slate.com/articles/sports/sports_nut/2013/01/rg3_knee _injury_what_a_shock_the_redskins_let_their_star_quarterback_play .html.

3. Klemko, "Dr. James Andrews."

4. JeramyRichter (YouTube user), "Mitt Romney & Obama on RG3 @ FOX NFL Sunday 10/21/12," YouTube.com, uploaded October 21, 2012, http://www.youtube.com/watch?v=VsbRMFgglf8.

5. Matt K. Lewis, "The Incredible Rise of Robert Griffin III," *The Week*,

October 28, 2012, http://theweek.com/bullpen/column/235366
/the-incredible-rise-of-robert-griffin-iii.

6. Tony Drovetto, "Pete Carroll on RGIII: 'When He's on, He's as Good as You Can Get,'" Seahawks.com, January 2, 2013, http://blog.seahawks.com/2013/01/02/pete-carroll-on-rgiii-when-hes-on-hes-as-good-as-you-can-get/.

7. Associated Press, "Seahawks Come Back from 14-0 Deficit to Beat Redskins; RG3 Hurt," NFL.com, January 7, 2013, http://www.nfl.com/news/story/0ap1000000123322/article/seahawks-come-back-from-140-deficit-to-beat-redskins-rg3-hurt.

8. Ibid.

9. Robert Griffin III, Twitter post, January 7, 2013, http://twitter.com/RGIII.

10. Russell Wilson, Twitter post, January 9, 2013, https://twitter.com/DangeRussWilson/status/289033887777185794.

ACKNOWLEDGMENTS

I'd like to thank my agent, Andrew Wolgemuth, for being a friend, an armchair therapist, a pro's pro, and (warning, cheesy sports analogy ahead) the most protective "left tackle" of an agent a writer could imagine having. You earn your percentage on every book, but you really earned it on this one.

To Terry Shea, Evan Sharpley, Jim Spiegel, Jim Kelly, and Eugene Lee for great interviews, and to Terry in particular for the inscribed copy of *Eyes Up*. Very cool.

To the friends with whom I share football: Cory Hartman, Peeter Lukas, Jean-Michel Hosdez and the St. Brieuc (France) Licornes, Jeff Skinner, Nathaniel Eyde, Norm Dufrin, Brian Erickson, and Tim "Coach" Cornman.

To Zach Bartels and Ronnie Martin for not knowing anything about football and not caring about this project at all. Sometimes not being asked about it was exactly what I needed.

A special shout-out to my pastoral types, who also double as armchair shrinks when I am at a certain delicate and always frustrating stage of the book publishing process—a stage during which I often say to them, "I'm never doing this again": Cory Hartman and Norm Dufrin.

To Dad, for all the football games, all the workouts, and all the conversations. To Tris and Maxim, my sons, for all your love.

To my students at Olivet College and Cornerstone University for not getting sick of me talking about this in class or, if you did get sick of it, not saying anything.

To the following books and/or pieces of media: chapters 7 and 8 of Paul's letter to the Romans, *Frank Sinatra's Greatest Hits* (Volume 2, vinyl), *Although of Course You End Up Becoming Yourself: A Road Trip with David Foster Wallace* by David Lipsky, *Counterfeit Gods* by Timothy Keller, and *Lust for Life: A Biographical Novel of Vincent Van Gogh* by Irving Stone.

Special thanks to Heather Skelton, Bryan Norman, Katherine Rowley, and especially Joel Miller at Thomas Nelson, for making this a smooth process from start to finish . . . and then the next finish.

Finally, the loudest of thanks to my sweet wife, Kristin Kluck, for the many hours of football she put up with for the duration of this project and, just kind of in general, in life. You're the best, baby, and I don't deserve you.

INDEX